FAULT LINES

INCEST, SEXUALITY AND CATHOLIC FAMILY CULTURE

WOMEN'S ISSUES PUBLISHING PROGRAM
SECOND STORY PRESS

FAULT LINES

INCEST, SEXUALITY AND CATHOLIC FAMILY CULTURE

by

Tish Langlois

WOMEN'S ISSUES PUBLISHING PROGRAM
SECOND STORY PRESS

SERIES EDITOR: BETH MCAULEY

CANADIAN CATALOGUING IN PUBLICATION DATA

Langlois, Tish, 1968–
Fault lines : incest, sexuality and Catholic family culture

Includes bibliographical references and index.
ISBN 0-929005-98-8

1. Incest - Religious aspects - Christianity.
2. Patriarchy - Religious aspects - Catholic church.
I. Title.

Edited by Beth McAuley
Copyedited by Doris Cowan

Front cover image (digitally manipulated):
Original photo by Canada Centre for Remote Sensing. Published in
Canada from Space by Camden House Publishing. Used with permission.

*Second Story Press gratefully acknowledges the support of the Ontario Arts
Council and the Canada Council for the Arts for our publishing program.*

Printed in Canada on acid-free, recycled paper

Published by
SECOND STORY PRESS
720 Bathurst Street, Suite 301
Toronto, Ontario
M5S 2R4

CONTENTS

*For the women who generously
shared their life stories with me and for all other
survivors of Catholic family culture.*

ACKNOWLEDGMENTS

MANY PEOPLE helped me bring this book into being. First on my list of people to thank are the women who participated in my study. I thank them for their courage, depthful insights and commitment.

I want to thank in a special way Beth McAuley (editor of *Fault Lines* as well as series and acquisitions editor of Second Story Press's Women's Issues Publishing Program) for her patience and dedication to this book project. I thank the women at Second Story Press for their professionalism and gentle encouragement as I moved toward my deadlines.

Thank you to those associated with the Women's Studies program at Memorial University, especially Barbara Neis and Joan Pennell for their unfailing support as my co-supervisors, Phyllis Artiss, Deborah Canning, Linda Kealey, Marilyn Porter, Joan Scott and Rosonna Tite.

I gratefully acknowledge two research grants received from Memorial University's Institute of Social and Economic Research (ISER). The institute funded the cost of research materials, three trips to the research site and the transcription of my interviews — thanks especially to Eleanor Fitzpatrick and James Tuck. I am also deeply grateful to those in Canada's religious communities who supported this important project.

Finally, a deeply felt thank-you to my family and circle of friends and colleagues for their inspiration and support: my parents, Sue and John Langlois; my sisters, Elizabeth and Nicole Langlois; and Jordan Bishop, Ann Louise Brookes,

Rhona Buchan, Moyra Buchan, Alice Collins, Sandra Cowan, Charmaine Davidge, Denis Deneau, Len Desroches, Sandra Everson, Janette Fecteau, Dolores Hall, Bernadette Hickey, Manrique Mata-Montero, Kelly Morris, Helen Murphy, John Arthur Murphy, Lindsay Myers, Elizabeth Oxlade, Kristy Piercey, Marlene Power, Geoffrey Newman, David A. Reid, Michelle A. Smith, Eugenia Sussex and William Sweet.

—Tish Langlois

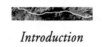

Introduction

THE RIGHT TIME IN HISTORY: EXPLORING SEXUAL JUSTICE

Sexual justice — the most trivialized, feared, and postponed dimension of social justice in western society and, possibly, in the world.[1]
— Harvard theologian Carter Heyward

WHEN WE THINK OF Catholicism, especially here in Newfoundland, sexual abuse is often not far from our minds. Revelations during the 1980s of child sexual abuse perpetrated against children by Catholic priests in the Archdiocese of St. John's, and by Christian Brothers at the Mount Cashel orphanage,[2] shocked and angered Newfoundland Catholics and non-Catholics alike. The sexual abuse crisis forced public attention on the need for change. People demanded answers. Among the most progressive responses were those that identified child sexual abuse as a gross misuse of social power. In a brief submitted by a special commission established to inquire into sexual abuse of children by members of clergy, for example, Newfoundland's Working Group on Child Sexual Abuse suggested that "power that is not open to challenge is ... dangerous and yet it is unchallenged power which the clergy in Newfoundland have enjoyed. And it is the issue of

power and control over others which is central to an understanding of sexual abuse — whether it occurs in nuclear families, the family of the church, or in non-family relationships."[3]

It wasn't long before reverberations from the sexual abuse
crisis reached the Canadian Catholic community at large.
Canadian bishops responded by establishing a working committee on clergy abuse of children. In their report, entitled
From Pain to Hope, they similarly stated that "child sexual
abuse flourishes in a society that is based on competition and
power and which is undermined by sexual exploitation and
violence against women."[4]

In September of 1993 — just three years after the Winter
Commission[5] released the findings from its inquiry into the
crisis — I arrived in Newfoundland to begin graduate work
in women's studies. I came as a feminist. I came as a Catholic.
I came as a person with a great interest not only in how to
reconcile these two realities in my own life but also in how
the Catholic church was responding to the enormous chal-
lenges it was facing over the issue of child sexual abuse. I
began to notice that many studies focused on sexual abuse
perpetrated by Catholic clergy — notably, sexual abuse of
male children — but that comparatively few studies sought to
explain incest,[6] that is, sexual abuse in Catholic family contexts. I decided to study an area that had been previously
under-explored by Canadian Catholics.

While the Catholic church's *official* position has always
promoted the dignity and value of all human beings, feminist
studies on social relations within the church and on Catholic
families reveal a long history of misogyny and abuse.[7] Many
feminists, in fact, consider Catholic teachings and practices to
be prime examples of patriarchal ideology.[8] Ideology, as I use
the term throughout this book, refers to those patriarchal
ideas, symbols and practices that underpin and sanction our

societal institutions, including our religious institutions. As I see it, one of the primary tasks for reflective Catholics is to differentiate between theology and ideology. Theology is about justice — what Carter Heyward calls the manifestation of God's love in the world.[9] Religious ideology, on the other hand, is about injustice — the use of religion to sanction and maintain unjust social relations.

Feminists have identified an extensive list of social factors relevant to Catholic patriarchal ideology: the disparagement of women's sexuality in historical and theological writings;[10] a theology of ownership that has historically protected men's proprietorship over women and children, including the right to violate women's and children's physical, sexual and emotional boundaries;[11] the exclusion of women from positions of leadership and authority within the church; projection of social evils onto secular society because it rejects traditional values;[12] and Catholicism's emphasis on suffering and self-sacrifice.[13] In the more specific case of Catholic family culture, some of these factors include Catholicism's emphasis on patriarchal authority, its historical support for women's subordination in the home, and, perhaps in a way that has least been explored to date, the way Catholicism has used the imagery of "Father God," ruling "His people" from "His heaven," to make the subordination of women and children seem natural and fitting.[14]

Collectively, we are learning that relationships that rely on the "rule of the father" foster a profound lack of mutuality among women and children who live with men. We are also learning that religious beliefs and practices are central to the formation of culture, and to the formation of gender and sexual relations (including incestuous relations) within that culture. Incest is arguably the most acute form of sexual oppression, first, because it involves a violation that is both sexual and physical, and second, because it occurs within families, where we normally look for protection from violation. And although research on incest is abundant, the role and impact of religion within incestuous relations is seldom considered.

In this book I examine gender and sexual relations through the eyes of Catholic incest survivors. I base my approach on feminist standpoint theory, an epistemology (derived from the Greek word *episteme,* meaning knowledge) grounded in the Hegelian and Marxist traditions. Standpoint theory assumes that individuals who both *experience* and *struggle against* oppression can provide a less distorted account of social reality than individuals who have an interest in maintaining the status quo. I conducted my research from the standpoint of Catholic women who have experienced and struggled against a particularly sinister sort of oppression, sexual abuse within their own families, because I believed that from their standpoint would emerge a clear and sound critique of Catholic family culture.

What I uncovered in my work with these women supports the findings of previous feminist research linking Christianity to sexual abuse.[15] The practices endorsed by Catholic family and sexual ideology, notably a gendered division of labour in families and a rigid regulation of sexuality, contributed to the disempowerment of women and children and, in turn, to the onset and continuation of incest.

When the best of Catholicism — that is, the requirement that we create a society that fosters the dignity of all its members — is applied to what we are learning about gender and sexual relations, we must ask to what extent traditional Catholic family values make this possible. In an attempt to answer this question, this book will examine how gender and sexual relations were socially constructed in eight Catholic families in which incest occurred, the extent to which Catholic family values and teachings played a role and, in turn, how these gender and sexual relations contributed to incest. The time period of the study (the 1940s to 1980s) also brings into focus some of the differences between Catholic family culture in the pre–Vatican II period and post–Vatican II period — a time of dramatic change in the Catholic church.

The Right Time in History: Point of Departure

In the fall of 1993, not long after my arrival in St. John's, Newfoundland, I visited St. John the Baptist Basilica on Military Road. I must have been an obvious newcomer, because a white-haired nun approached me and invited me to tea at one of the convents next door. (I must also look like potential convent material — I've been approached by nuns on a number of occasions!) Several nuns, mostly older women, joined us, and I happily answered their questions about my family and studies at the university. I engaged them in conversation about the Catholic church's response to the sexual abuse crisis, and told them I intended to write a thesis about sexual abuse in Catholic families. These were clearly very difficult topics for them, but, being somewhat foolhardy and persistent, I took the opportunity to examine their assumptions about how and why incest occurs. Having already formulated some theories about how Catholicism might play a role in incest, I argued that incest occurs in families where there is an imbalance of power between women and men, where there is shame about sexuality, and where women are economically vulnerable (all characteristics commonly found in Catholic families). "Oh, no, no, no, dear! That's just not so!" they replied in unison. I left the convent profoundly struck by their collective resistance to the idea that any truly Catholic man would abuse a female relative. They believed that any man who sexually abuses a female relative is simply *personally* deficient: not respectful enough, not good enough; in short, if he did such a thing, it was not because he was Catholic, but because he was not Catholic *enough*. I was concerned about their unquestioning acceptance of Catholicism and their assumption that a truly *Catholic* man would be, ipso facto, incapable of committing incest. After our meeting I wondered if they would think about what I had said, and I became even more determined to examine the roots of incest in Catholic families.

The beliefs about incest expressed by these sisters may be widely shared among Roman Catholics, as I discovered shortly after giving a CBC interview in December of 1994 on my research-in-progress. An article published in Newfoundland's Catholic journal *The Monitor*, the following February, outlined a local commentator's opposition to CBC's decision to air this interview. He described the interview as an "abuse of journalistic privilege." What especially intrigued me about his opposition to my research was his belief that among Catholic family members who have an inclination toward incest, "it is precisely their Catholic faith which prevents them from sinning."[16] I suspected that this man's statement was representative of a widespread assumption that sexual abuse is simply the result of an individual lack of self-control rather than societal structures and practices — including religious ones — that foster relations of dominance and subordination. I was also concerned about his unquestioning assumptions, first, that Catholicism in no way encourages imbalances of social power, and second, that *faith* is enough to protect a person against engaging in sexually abusive acts. His statement affected me in a similar way to my meeting with the sisters: it spurred my determination to explore the relationship between Catholicism, sexuality and abusive gender relations.

I arrived in Newfoundland at the right time in history — my own history and the social history within Canada's Catholic community — to respond to child sexual abuse in Catholic families.[17] In retrospect, my decision to tackle this very thorny and taboo subject was supported by my history as a reflective, justice-minded Catholic and as a woman responsive to and involved in the second wave of feminist activism. I hoped I could break ground in a new area of social/sexual justice.

I learned social justice principles from my parents. Their social activism was solidly grounded in the context of their faith, notably the social teachings of the Catholic church. This tradition of social teaching "calls" us (in the Catholic sense of "vocation") to be critical of dominant trends in our society and emphasizes the need to transform unjust structures and institutions.[18] For my parents, social justice was (at least from my view looking back at their work) a set of principles informed by faith, demanding action to change an unjust world.

I took an interest in Catholic social teaching from an early age. I was an earnest, thoughtful and spiritual child. The rituals, symbols and teachings of my Catholic upbringing captured my imagination. (My grandmother once told me a story about having witnessed me, at the age of about six or seven, solemnly lighting a candle after mass — evidence, she thought, of my spiritual and reflective nature.) One of my earliest associations with Catholicism is of attending mass at St. Rita's Parish in Woodstock, Ontario. I loved attending mass at St. Rita's because the choir sang what was, to my young ears, a beautiful and moving rendition of the Lamb of

God prayer. The words — "Lamb of God, you take away the sin of the world. Have mercy on us. Lamb of God, you take away the sin of the world. Have mercy on us. Lamb of God, you take away the sin of the world. Grant us your peace" — inspired in me a sense that it was also *our* task to take away the sin of the world. Even at that young age, I had already learned that "the sin of the world" didn't refer to petty individual sins (as many Catholics were apt to believe). Rather, "sin" was a political notion. Sin referred to social sin — social injustice.

When I was a small child, my parents' social justice work centred on the Canadian Catholic Organization for Development and Peace. CCODP was established in the late 1960s and continues to have one of the most political voices within the Canadian Catholic church. The organization focuses on issues of structural economic injustice, especially imbalances of First World greed and Third World poverty. In later years my parents' activism primarily took the form of work among rural people in Southwestern Ontario, promoting and fostering land stewardship and solidarity among farmers and farming families. They formed political lobbies to fight for fairer prices for farm commodities and for marketing systems that would guarantee farming families a just return for their labour. I valued and respected the work they did. Today I am proud to say that my introduction to political activism and critical thinking included access to such revolutionary texts as Paulo Freire's *Pedagogy of the Oppressed*.[19]

While I was profoundly influenced by my parents' commitment to faith-centred social activism, I was also influenced by their beliefs about sexuality. I suspect that my experience was like that of many other Catholic children of that era. As far as I can tell, when it came to sexuality my parents lived their lives by the rules they learned as children and young adults during the pre–Vatican II era (that is, before the mid-1960s) when Catholicism was characterized by rigorous moral codes, especially regarding sexuality. Because of this, it was a struggle for us as children to express our sexuality. We were constrained by the fact that any expression of sexuality outside the safe and "proper" context of marriage was deemed immoral and inappropriate, or at the very least, made everyone very uncomfortable. We were inadvertently and unintentionally taught to fear sexuality. I do not blame my parents for this; they were brought up in an era of erotophobia — a fear of sexuality that Catholicism seems to exaggerate and encourage — as were their parents, and so on back through many previous generations.[20]

I suspect my parents were, like most justice-minded Catholics in the 1970s, not consciously concerned with *sexual* justice as I use the term in this book. The notion really hadn't yet emerged. The idea of sexual justice, a recently recognized and previously unexplored dimension of social justice, has emerged largely as a response to the consciousness-raising of second-wave feminism, with its close analysis of oppressive gender and sexual relations. While faith-centred social justice activism has traditionally worked to correct large-scale economic injustices, such as the exploitation of labour and global disparities in standards of living, sexual justice is a call to link patterns of gender and sexual injustice to those of economic, political and racial injustice. Carter Heyward, writing at the close of the 1980s, identified sexual justice as "the most trivialized, feared, and postponed dimension of social justice in western society and, possibly, in the world."[21] It is sexual justice that I am primarily concerned with in this book — exploring the dimensions of sexual justice as they relate to both Catholic family culture and social justice activism. To *practice* sexual justice in our society, especially for women, means struggling against various forms of ideology, perhaps especially religious ideology. The stories I document in this book can give us important insights as we continue our common search for sexual justice.

Growing up during the height of second-wave feminism, I found it an easy transition in my thinking to apply what I had learned about justice and political activism to work among women. My own explorations of sexual justice (though I hadn't yet consciously named it as such) began in the late 1980s. As a university undergraduate and a young feminist in the women's movement I absorbed a key tenet of second-wave feminism, "the personal is political," which came out of the sexual politics debate of the 1960s and 1970s.[22] This tenet led to one of the great achievements of second-wave feminism: the politicization of gender and sexual relations within the so-called private sphere. Concurrently, I read the works of great feminist writers and became inspired by feminist activists who were busy bringing about personal/political change in their own lives and communities. Thus, while I became familiar with the scholarly feminist literature on such topics as sexual assault, domestic violence and incest, I began to meet women who had personally experienced these injustices. In my early undergraduate days, I also studied theology, and so, during a course on Catholicism's theology of marriage and "the family"[23] I learned — and raged to my friends — about a theology that upheld precisely those gender and sexual arrangements that feminists were criticizing!

In my twenties, I continued to integrate what I was learning from "secular feminism" about gender and sexual politics with what I knew about faith-centred social activism. By the time I began my master's degree in 1993, I was ready to begin a critique of Catholicism's official (that is, theologically

approved) doctrine on marriage, family life and sexuality, focusing on the obvious gap I perceived between Catholic social justice teaching and Catholic teaching on "the family." I
suspected that if Catholic social justice were to take seriously
into account a feminist analysis of gender and sexual relations, the ramifications for Catholic teachings on marriage
and family life would be obvious, immediate and deep.

At the same time, I perceived a gap between academic
feminism and spirituality. I was a faith-centred feminist
working within a predominantly atheist academic milieu; I
was aware of walking boundaries of feminist theory and feminist activism that didn't easily accommodate my faith-centred
commitments. But I didn't apologize for incorporating these
commitments into my academic work. Spiritual commitments often provide the foundation for political commitments. I was clear that my denunciation of Catholic ideology
was not a repudiation of spirituality, nor a rejection of all aspects of Catholic teaching. I was strongly connected to the
Catholic tradition and believed many of its principles could
strengthen feminist activism. In other words, I felt that
Catholic social justice teaching and feminism had a lot to
learn from and to teach each other.[24]

So it wasn't surprising to me when, one day in the spring
of 1994, I awoke from a dream reciting to myself this mantra:
"My research is grounded in my experiences of the divine." I
didn't fully know what it meant at the time but I knew it was
important. At that point in the history of my graduate program I was really wrestling with how to integrate these strong
commitments to feminism and to spirituality. As I reflect on
the dream mantra today, I am keenly aware that there was,
and continues to be, a vital, creative tension at work in me. It
is a tension between questioning Catholic teachings on "the
family" and respecting and valuing Catholicism's commitment

to social justice. In other words, it is a tension between criticizing the disempowering aspects of Catholicism and valuing what I learned from my upbringing as the best of Catholicism: a belief in a divine creator who wants the best for her/his creatures; a recognition that people are more valuable than things or material wealth; the formal (if not always actual) commitment to sharing the earth's resources for the common good; the value of common worship and ritual; the power of forgiveness; and a sense that although the world is often a brutal and conflict-filled place, the principles of social justice call us to strive to transform it.

THEORETICAL FRAMEWORK AND METHODOLOGY

Throughout the writing of this book I was guided by a socialist feminist analysis that places importance on the socio-economic status of women in families within a capitalist, patriarchal society. By using a socialist feminist analysis to explore sexual justice I mean to encourage readers (Catholic or non-Catholic) to examine how our society's foundational assumptions about marriage, monogamy and heterosexuality have been socially constructed in ways that sanction and maintain patriarchal relations. My socialist feminist critique of the gender and sexual relations endorsed by Catholic ideology sets up an exploration of how gender and sexual relations might become more empowering for women and children in Catholic families.

My analysis is guided in special ways by the insights of feminist standpoint theorists. It was in my final undergraduate year that I became familiar with feminist standpoint epistemologies, especially those of Sandra Harding and Dorothy E. Smith.[25] Harding and Smith argue that women's experiences of marginalization and oppression make women's lives epistemically privileged starting-points for sociological research. According to standpoint theorists, those who are oppressed can "know" the social world in a less partial way than those who have an interest in maintaining the status quo. Smith argues that much of what is perceived as knowledge (or truth) in our society is actually the ideology of a ruling group. The ruling group in our patriarchal, capitalist, heterosexist society is composed primarily of white heterosexual males, and thus ruling ideology reflects their interests. It therefore becomes the task of the oppressed (for example, incest survivors) to expose what those in ruling groups call *knowledge* about the world (for example, that traditional, patriarchal families offer children the best chance of finding security and happiness) as *ideology* — that which reinforces the dominance of a ruling group.

As the Catholic church is a male-dominated institution, the set of ideas, symbols and practices it promotes stands as an example of society's larger patriarchal ideology. The ideological character of Catholic family culture becomes visible through emergent "lines of fault" in women's lives.[26] On one side of the fault lines are Catholic texts and practices; on the other side of the fault lines are women's experiences of oppression. Thus, I explore the contrast between *idealized* Catholic family life as depicted in official Catholic writings and Catholic families as *actually experienced* by incest survivors.

I was attracted by the fact that both Harding and Smith are grounded in the Marxist tradition and sought to make links between feminist standpoint theory and Christian social justice teachings — teachings that have also been influenced by the Marxist tradition. In the early days of my master's program I therefore set about weaving together the common principles of feminist standpoint theory and social justice activism. The most important commonalities are their shared beliefs that we live in an unjust world — a world that calls us to action and social change — and that by looking to the experiences of those who experience injustice, we can best learn how to change the world.

As a way of conducting feminist research that begins from the standpoint of women, I used a qualitative, participatory action methodology. Participatory action methodologies are different from traditional methodologies in which the researcher is the "expert" and attempts to maintain an "objective" position *vis-à-vis* the research subjects. Instead, participatory methodologies make research participants central, not peripheral, actors in the discovery process. The local women's centre in the town in which I conducted the research assisted me in identifying participants. Over a two-and-a-half-year period, eight women participated in the study. I met with them three times individually and twice as a group.[27]

This action-oriented methodology was compatible with my social justice orientation and allowed us to explore ways of changing gender and sexual relations — in short, we explored ways of bringing about sexual justice. I hope my theoretical framework and methodology enabled me to write a book that honours the lives and intentions of the women who so generously shared their life stories with me. This was my intent.

A "ROAD-MAP" FOR READERS

The women whose life stories are told throughout this book are introduced in the first chapter. I provide an overview of their incest histories and families. I then describe how their collaboration with me in a participatory action methodology guided this exploration of incest in Catholic families.

In Chapter 2 I explain the theoretical framework that guides the analysis in the rest of the book. I introduce key theoretical concepts such as socialist feminism and feminist standpoint theory, and begin to apply the theoretical framework to the case of Catholic family culture.

Chapter 3 provides definitions of incest and some theories that try to explain its occurrence. I place incest within a larger social context, notably the socio-economic realities of mothering in our society, in order to deepen our understanding of how and why incest occurs.

As I show in Chapter 4, I am not the first to provide a critique of religious ideology. In recent years, several feminist scholars have opened up the debate. My goal in Chapter 4 is to help the reader better understand Catholic family culture in the twentieth century by looking at ways that the Catholic church has, throughout history, shaped gender and sexual relations in western culture.

In Chapter 5 I take a historical materialist approach as I begin to chart the fault lines in Catholic families — the contradictions between Catholic family life as it was idealized between the 1940s and 1980s and the actualities of everyday/everynight life as it was lived in Catholic families during those decades. I also explore the conditions that permitted these women, at various moments in history, to identify themselves as incest survivors .

Male privilege in families, a key component of Catholic family ideology, is explored in Chapter 6. Through this exploration we learn how male privilege inspired a fear of male authority among these incest survivors and made it difficult if not impossible for them to challenge their abusers.

In Chapter 7 I continue to explore Catholic family ideology, this time looking at the role of mothering in Catholic families. When examined carefully, the women's stories encourage us to remove blame from the shoulders of mothers and instead to explore how Catholic ideology demanded that mothers give precedence to their roles as "good" Catholic wives and mothers over their own and their daughters' well-being.

Chapter 8 explores links between incest and Catholic sexual ideology — expressed in the plethora of Catholic rules that regulated sexuality and rewarded sexual purity. The women's stories illustrate how Catholic family culture, characterized by silence, fear and shame about sexuality, compounded their experiences of incest.

In the final chapter, the women share their visions for the transformation of Catholic family culture. They talk about their struggle to bring about sexual justice in their own lives and families. Their collective standpoint strengthens contemporary critiques of Catholic teachings on marriage, sexuality and family life and contributes in vital ways to the dialogue between feminism and the Catholic social justice tradition.

AN INVITATION

This book is not intended to be the last word on the subject of Catholic family culture and social/sexual justice. As Len Desroches points out in *Allow the Water,* his recent book on the spirituality and practice of Christian non-violence,[28] dialogue about — and a common search for — social/sexual justice is urgently needed. This book is intended as a contribution to that dialogue. For readers familiar with Catholicism, it will undoubtedly inspire a range of emotions and opinions; for women readers, I hope it will resonate with your experiences as women in a capitalist, patriarchal society; for those readers who are incest survivors, I hope it provides some measure of support and hope. And for those readers for whom all three realities converge, I hope this book is especially thought-provoking and affirming. To these and any other readers, I extend an invitation to explore with me the complex realities of incest, sexuality and Catholic family culture.

Participants' Biographical Overviews

Four of the women were brought up prior to Vatican II (pre–1960s):

ELIZABETH

- born 1937
- French-Canadian ancestry
- raised in northern Ontario
- one of ten children in family of origin
- sexually abused by family acquaintance, father and brother
- married, divorced, annulled
- recalled memories of abuse in mid-1980s
- mother of several children
- mother of sexually abused children

CHERRIE

- born 1943
- lived in orphanage between ages one and three
- adopted in 1947 by family of Scottish ancestry
- raised in rural Nova Scotia
- one of four children in adoptive family
- sexually abused by father and two brothers
- married, divorced, annulled
- recalled memories of abuse in mid-1980s
- mother of one

FAYE

- born 1944
- Irish and Lithuanian ancestry
- raised in Irish Catholic community of Liverpool, England
- one of two children in family of origin
- sexually abused by father
- married, divorced, annulled
- began to recall memories of abuse around 1990
- entered a religious congregation; left before final profession

MARY

- born 1945
- mixed Scottish, Irish and French ancestry
- raised in rural Cape Breton Island
- fourth of seven children in family of origin
- sexually abused by father
- recalled repressed memories around 1990

- married and mother of several children
- daughter sexually abused by Mary's father
- Mary's father also a survivor of sexual abuse by a male relative

The other four women were brought up in the era of Vatican II Catholicism:

COURAGE
- born 1960
- mixed Irish and Scottish ancestry
- raised in a predominantly Catholic Nova Scotia town
- one of six children in family of origin
- emotionally and physically abused by both parents
- sexually abused by aunt
- began to recall repressed memories of sexual abuse in 1990
- married, divorced
- mother of several children

MAYA
- born 1965
- mixed French-Canadian and Polish ancestry
- raised in rural Nova Scotia
- third of six children in family of origin
- sexually abused by uncle
- single, no plans to marry

CONTENT
- born 1967
- Scottish and Cape Breton French ancestry
- raised in rural Nova Scotia
- eighth of twelve children in family of origin
- sexually abused by an older brother
- engaged to be married

JACKIE
- born 1969
- Scottish and Acadian French ancestry
- raised in rural Nova Scotia
- three children in family of origin
- sexually abused by stepfather
- lives with her partner

Chapter 1

KNOWLEDGE IN THE MAKING: WOMEN'S EXPERIENCES OF THE RESEARCH PROCESS

I really liked your feminist approach where you tried to reduce as much as possible the power differential between researcher and subjects. And I liked the way you saw it as a collaborative enterprise. You were doing this as a researcher but there was a solidarity there as a researcher, we weren't just people you were examining in a very objective way. I think it's much more humane than the old way of keeping [the research process] objective and non-involved. So I didn't feel just like a subject in an experiment but more of a kind of co-creator in this work.   — Faye

I feel really good about the process. I think it was really care-ful, as in full-of-care. You know, it was really respectful and there was every opportunity to have input. I feel good about that. If those measures hadn't been taken I probably wouldn't have felt as comfortable with the whole thing.   — Maya

EARLY IN MY STUDY, largely in response to both the scholarly attention being paid to Catholic clergy abuse of male children in Newfoundland and the lack of attention being paid to the sexual abuse of girls in Catholic family contexts, I decided to research incest in Catholic families. When I designed my research methodology I had several goals. First, I wanted to conduct research *from the standpoint of women*[1] (I discuss feminist standpoint theory in greater detail in Chapter 2) — for I was convinced that the standpoint of Catholic incest survivors would provide a strong and sound critique of gender and sexual relations in Catholic families. I knew that, while my voice and analysis as a Catholic feminist would be important, the voices of the incest survivors would take front and centre stage — *their experiences* and *their struggles* would provide the foundation for the study.

A second goal was to make my research an example of *feminist praxis* — the joining of theory and action in order to challenge gender and sexual oppression. To do this, I took an alternative research approach, a participatory approach in which the research participants became, with me, *co-creators* of knowledge about Catholic family culture. My goal was to conduct research that would contribute not only to social change and women's empowerment in a broad sense but also to the empowerment of the participants at every stage of the research process.[2]

Finally, as a Catholic feminist, I wanted to integrate into my methodology the principles of social justice that call us to transform unjust structures and practices. By exploring unjust gender and sexual relations in Catholic families I knew I would be contributing to the important dialogue about *sexual justice* — to date, one of the least explored dimensions of social justice in western society.[3]

The Participant Group

I conducted the research within a small community in Nova Scotia. My main reason for selecting this community as the research site was its predominantly Catholic population. Another important consideration was the fact that I had some connections with the feminist network in that community. When I met with the women's centre staff about my research plans they were enthusiastic and agreed to distribute a summary of my research objectives (see Appendix I) among the participants in two local groups for survivors of sexual abuse. They also agreed to distribute the summary to two feminist counsellors in town. I didn't have a definite number of participants in mind, although I knew I needed at least four, and I hoped that more than four women would volunteer. As it turned out, I was correct in assuming that my links with the existing feminist network would help me to build a strong and successful participatory action methodology. Within ten days I had secured a list of eight possible participants, all of whom eventually agreed to join my research group.

I contacted each of them by phone, and after I had told them more about myself and the kind of research I intended to do, all but one (Faye, who wanted more information about the project) agreed to participate. I sent Faye a copy of my research proposal and, after reading it, she too enthusiastically agreed to participate. She told me, "I can remember when I first read the proposal, feeling a bit shocked. It was almost as if you were attacking my mother, the church. But once I kind of got over that feeling I was impressed with your proposal and it really started me thinking."

I was aware that research with women survivors of sexual abuse would present me with a number of serious ethical concerns. Indeed, survivors of sexual abuse are considered a vulnerable population because they have been selected on account of their incest histories,[4] and I sought to protect them in several ways. The most important way was ensuring that the participants had access to therapeutic resources throughout the research period. In other words, I stipulated in my summary of research objectives that I would invite to join the study only women who were active in a group for survivors of sexual abuse, or who were seeing a counsellor, or who were doing both.[5]

It was quite by chance that two distinct groups of participants emerged, and I only realized this after the first set of individual interviews. Four of the women — Elizabeth, Cherrie, Faye and Mary — were in their late forties or early fifties at the time that I began the study. So these women were brought up, for the most part, during the 1940s and 1950s in Catholic families that were strongly influenced by strict *pre–Vatican II* Catholicism.

The other group of women — Courage, Maya, Content and Jackie — were in their twenties or thirties when the study began. So, for the most part, their stories reflect life in Catholic families during the time of *post–Vatican II* Catholicism — after the mid-1960s — a time not only of dramatic change within the Catholic church but also of second-wave feminism.

The names that appear in this book are not the women's actual names. They chose their own pseudonyms, in most cases names that had special meaning for them. I purposely asked them to do this in the hope that this would prove to be a small but significant way for them to take ownership of their role in the study. At the conclusion of the study, when I asked Jackie whether it had been significant to choose her own pseudonym, she told me:

At first I didn't think it was important to choose my own pseudonym. But then I was glad, it was more personalized than you just saying, "Okay you're going to be known as so-and-so." It wasn't as cold. You know, when you read other accounts of people's work and they say, "I will use so-and-so," and then in quotations, "not the real person's name," you often wonder, "Well, how does that person *feel*"? So for me it was important.

When I asked Courage to reflect on the significance of her pseudonym, she had this to say:

> I chose that name because it's taken a lot of courage to look inside and do as much work as I've done on myself. Looking honestly at your life is scary — looking at why I became the way I did, why I became an addict, why I did the things I did. It took a hell of a lot of courage to turn my life around and to find a way of teaching my children to live that's different from what I learned.

In the following pages I introduce the eight women who were the central actors in our critique of Catholic family culture and production of a new understanding of Catholic family life.

ELIZABETH

Elizabeth was born in 1937 into a French-Canadian family. One of ten children, she grew up in a rural community in Northern Ontario. She emphasized that her parents were formed in "the pre–Vatican II era [of the church] and re-mained faithful to those Catholic teachings" throughout their lives — including the church's teachings on gender roles in the family. She noted that while the changes after Vatican II gave her family members the freedom "to express themselves a little differently, a little more freely, at the same time they clung to the basic Catholic values they had learned in that pre–Vatican II era." In 1957 she married "an indifferent Catholic" and assumed sole responsibility for bringing up her children as Catholics. "I did that much more out of a sense of duty than desire — which was sort of the norm in those pre–Vatican II days." She and her husband eventually separated, divorced and received an annulment from the Catholic church. Elizabeth identifies the mid-1980s, when she uncovered memories of her history both of sexual abuse by a family acquaintance, and of incest with her father and brother, as a time of profound change for her. "Uncovering that history of abuse was really life-changing — I couldn't look at *anything* the same way again." Today Elizabeth "no longer act[s] out of a sense of unworthiness and shame — which is a real accomplishment." She also continues to take to a deeper level her understanding both of the role of the Catholic church in her incest history and the role of faith and spirituality in her healing. "There's a lot of empowerment that, for me, has come through reflecting on the trauma and integrating my life — through the healing process I was able to put the pieces of my life back together. I no longer feel the need to act out of the fragments. I act out of my wholeness."

CHERRIE

Cherrie was born in 1943, and at the age of one, when her birth mother decided to give her up for adoption, she went to live in an orphanage. In 1947, at the age of three and half, she was adopted by a family that lived in a predominantly

Catholic rural community in Nova Scotia. When I asked her to reflect on ways that her adoptive family was a Catholic family she said, "Well, everything was pretty rigid in those days. We said the family rosary at least once a day and we went to mass as a family and were encouraged to go to daily mass during Lent and Advent. We always observed the days of fasting and abstinence and the feast days of the church too." Cherrie, the only daughter and the youngest of four children, was sexually abused by her father and two of her brothers. In her forties the incest memories surfaced and she began the healing process that has so strongly shaped her life in the past decade. "As far as I can remember the incest began with my father, not too long after I moved into the home. I only have two memories of that abuse, which means that as far as I know it only happened twice. But when I turned five, the abuse began with two of my brothers. Eventually the abuse was just happening with one of my brothers and that continued until I was thirteen. I still have difficulty remembering huge chunks of my childhood so there certainly could be more abuse that I've forgotten." Cherrie married in her early twenties and has a son from this marriage. Some years into her marriage Cherrie and her husband divorced and eventually received an annulment from the Catholic church. About her spiritual life, Cherrie said, "I've always had a deep faith. Even as a small child the Blessed Mother was a strong presence in my life and she was always a source of comfort. I've been given the gift of faith and it keeps growing — my faith is really the thing that has guided my healing process."

FAYE

One of two children, Faye was born in 1944 to parents of Irish and Lithuanian descent. She was raised in the Irish Catholic community of Liverpool, England, where Catholicism was inextricably tied to national and cultural identity. She told me, "The Irish Catholic influence was very strong. I don't think I even met a Protestant until I went to university. I may have met them in stores but not socially. I went to Catholic schools, I went to Catholic dances and belonged to Catholic clubs — *everything* was in a Catholic context." Her parents upheld the tenets of the pre–Vatican II Catholic church and stayed together "through thick and thin." Faye was sexually abused by her father from a very early age, until about the age of twelve. Partly as an act of rebellion against the incest, Faye rejected the Catholic church for many years. She married a Protestant and emigrated to Canada with her husband where she pursued post-secondary studies in psychology. After several years of marriage they divorced. Faye chose not to have any children. "One of the big reasons is that, although I didn't have conscious memories of the incest at the time, I was aware that my own childhood had been really horrifying and traumatic." In her late thirties Faye returned to the Catholic church and some years later joined an order of Catholic nuns. She left the order before final profession of vows, but it was during those five years that she began to remember the abuse. She now maintains her own practice as a psychologist and specializes in the area of child sexual abuse. Faye is critical of many Catholic teachings and practices yet she remains within the church. She does so in part to promote her own healing, but also to bring about healing within the church itself — a church that is "pretty messed up when it comes to sexuality and dealing with sexual sin."

MARY

Mary was born in 1945, the fourth of seven children, into a Cape Breton family of mixed Scottish, Irish and French ancestry. Her family's social activity revolved around the church life of her family's rural parish. She told me her daily life was permeated by the influence of Catholicism: "You're talking to someone who went to daily mass a lot of my life and especially through high school. And I used to be at choir practice with my parents when most children were at home in bed — my mother played the organ and my father was choir director so they'd be there for hours. Everything was in Latin in those days so I know my Latin inside and out. But it was also the religion we got at home and in school. Catholicism was *everywhere*. So those circumstances are what helped form me. I don't mean to imply that it was all a negative experience. In fact, I think there was a way that it gave me comfort. I'm sure I saw attending mass, for example, as a kind of purification ritual. It was me looking for a relationship with God, to be sure, but in hindsight it was also me trying to find a way to atone for the 'sins' of my past. It wasn't a conscious memory of the incest but it was an overall sense of feeling unworthy. And that feeling, I know now, came from the experience of being sexually abused." Mary was sexually abused by her father from the time she was "still in the crib" until age twelve. Her repressed memories of incest began to surface in 1990 when her daughter disclosed that she also had been sexually abused by Mary's father. The generational cycles of sexual violence in Mary's family go back at least three generations; shortly after Mary confronted him, Mary's father disclosed that he too had been sexually abused in childhood by a male relative. Mary's healing has been strengthened by many things, including her involvement in the feminist movement

and her faith. She is critical of the Catholic church and ad-
mits there are tensions to being a feminist *and* a Catholic.
"To dare to be a feminist you can't maintain the status quo all
the time. But being a Catholic has traditionally meant following a set path — so for me there is definitely some tension."
It is her hope that she will be able to remain within the
church, in part because she feels a strong need to call priests
to become sensitized and educated about incest and sexual
abuse.

COURAGE

One of six children, Courage was born in 1960 into a family
of mixed Irish and Scottish ancestry. She grew up in a predominantly Catholic community in Nova Scotia. A survivor
of physical and emotional abuse by both parents, Courage
was also sexually abused by her aunt for many years. She told
me that her day-to-day life as a child was filled with abuse.
"My parents were good Catholics, at least they went to
church every Sunday and all that. But there was so much
abuse and shame — my whole life was about shame. I blame
society for the shame, I blame the church and I blame my
parents, too. When I first started to work on myself I gave the
shame back. I realized it wasn't mine to begin with." She is a
recovering alcoholic and drug addict who identifies her alcohol and drug dependence prior to 1990 as the primary way
she suppressed the pain of her childhood. Detailed memories
of her incest history began to surface about a year after she
gained sobriety. Although Courage rejects the official
Catholic church, a vital part of her healing has been her
strong relationship with God. "Today, the God of my understanding is loving and shows me different things as I need

them. When I ask God for strength I feel stronger. And it's not a priest or anyone else telling me I have to do this — it's me that wants to receive it." Courage became pregnant as a teenager and was pressured into a Catholic marriage. She is now a divorced single parent. During our final interview she said she hopes that telling her story will enable her to reach people with similar life histories. "Even if just one person says, 'Hey, this person was sexually abused, she was an addict — but she made it. Maybe I can too!' it will have been worth it."

MAYA

The third of six children, Maya was born in 1965 into a family of mixed French-Canadian and Polish ancestry. She grew up in a rural community in Nova Scotia. Between the ages of seven and twelve Maya was sexually abused by her father's youngest brother. During our interviews, Maya also identified some "serious issues around sexuality" with her father. Maya told me: "I'd say my parents' world-view was at least 75 per cent determined by the fact that they were Catholic. My parents' way of thinking was: 'If there's a hierarchy in heaven — of God the father as head and everyone else sort of trickling down in this big structure — then that must be the right way for things to be here on earth.' The ideal was the father as this benevolent ruler and his power was supposed to be a good thing but in my family Dad's power was based on fear rather than respect — and he abused his power. So when I was being abused there was no way I was going to ask him for help. I would've just been blamed and punished." In recent years Maya began counselling specifically related to her history of incest and she told me that participating in this study moved her to "unequivocally identify [her]self as an incest survivor." She feels the family dynamics that enabled the incest in her family were due in large part to Catholicism. She is critical of many Catholic teachings and practices — especially ones relating to sexuality — though she is still comfortable identifying with the Catholic church. Maya is a freelance writer and editor. She is single and has no plans to marry.

CONTENT

Content was born in 1966, the eighth of twelve children, into a family of mixed Scottish and Cape Breton French ancestry. She was sexually abused by an older brother between the ages of nine and twelve. While she describes her now-deceased parents as having been "not staunchly Catholic," she nevertheless emphasized that they upheld basic Catholic teachings — such as those opposing premarital sex and contraception. She also stressed that the gender roles taken on by her parents were traditional. "My mother was a very meek kind of person. It seems that in all my memories of her she was in the kitchen — doing 'women's work.' I hate that term, 'women's work.'" Content told me that her history of incest primarily undermined her self-confidence and made her very fearful of men. "Having been abused, I was always scared away from relationships. Who knows? If I hadn't been so scared I might have had a high school sweetheart kind of thing. Instead I had to do a lot of therapy and work on myself before I was able to have a healthy relationship." Content, who has been actively healing from her history of incest for several years, is now "content" with her life. She is engaged to be married.

JACKIE

Jackie was born in 1969 into a single-parent family of Scottish and French-Canadian ancestry. She was raised in a rural community in Nova Scotia. Several years after Jackie was born, her mother married and had three other children. Jackie was physically and sexually abused by her stepfather for most of her childhood years. She describes her mother and stepfather as "strong Catholics" who were committed to weekly attendance at mass. She told me, "Everybody really liked my stepfather. I know that our neighbours thought of us as this nice, Catholic family. At least that's the way we were perceived. We went to church every Sunday and I remember thinking that if I ever told people what my stepfather was doing to me they would probably say, 'How could such a good Catholic man do something like that? He's raising a family, he's a good provider...' So for me there was this huge fear of not being believed. And, you know, the funny thing is that I just didn't have a label for what was happening to me. It was something you'd see on a TV show and say, 'My God, that's awful.' But it certainly wasn't something that happened to anyone *we* knew! It didn't happen in traditional families like ours, it only happened in strange and abnormal families." During Jackie's teenage years her mother and stepfather separated and divorced. Jackie's healing process got under way when she became involved with the women's support group at her university. "It was important for me to be involved in that support group because it was during my four years of university that I really explored the issues. For the first time I had a safe place to talk about what I'd gone through — and for the first time in my life I realized the abuse wasn't my fault. I didn't have to worry about people judging me or not believing me. I was basically anonymous in that group but before that, in my community, I was really scared that people would find out and that I'd damage my family's reputation. It was also that good Catholic children just weren't supposed to question their parents. The women's group allowed me to vent my anger and they taught me that it was okay to be angry. After that I was finally able to get on with my healing." Today Jackie feels she has reached a sense of closure in her healing. But she doesn't want to turn her back on the healing process. "If I hadn't gone through the healing, I wouldn't be the person I am today." Jackie lives with her partner and hopes to have children some day.

PARTICIPATORY ACTION RESEARCH: "A RADICAL ALTERNATIVE TO KNOWLEDGE PRODUCTION"[6]

The life stories of these eight women and their participation in the research process shaped our critique of Catholic family culture in radical and powerful ways. Our process, in accordance with our feminist participatory action methodology, challenged many traditional assumptions about doing social research. As a *feminist* methodology, participatory action research assumes that we live in a world that is oppressive to women. As a *participatory* methodology, it assumes that those with whom the research is being conducted ought to play a vital role in the production of knowledge. And, as an *action-oriented* methodology, it assumes that an important goal of research is social change. For decades, social scientists, and especially feminist social scientists, have been working out research methodologies that are more participatory, inclusive and emancipatory than traditional, mainstream methodologies. In *Doing Participatory Research: A Feminist Approach*, Patricia Maguire distinguishes between two research paradigms, the traditional, or mainstream, approach to social research, and the alternative, participatory approach:

> The dominant approach to social science research has been called "traditional," "orthodox," "mainstream," or "classical" [and] refers to research grounded in positivism, the view that recognizes only positive facts and observable, "objective" phenomena. The pervasiveness and often unquestioned acceptance of positivist-informed research cuts us off from serious consideration of alternative assumptions and subsequent approaches to the production of social knowledge ... Participatory research is based on a set of assumptions about the nature of society and about social science research that is directly opposed to the assumptions of the dominant, positivist-informed, social science research. Participatory research offers a critique of, and challenge to, dominant positivist social science research as the only legitimate and valid source of knowledge. It provides a radical alternative to knowledge production.[7]

In the mainstream view, the social researcher is supposed to aim at discovering basic scientific facts or relationships but not get directly involved in linking social research to action. And the mainstream view assumes that it is up to the researcher, and not those on whom the research is conducted, to make these discoveries. By contrast, the alternative approach makes the participants central actors, not passive subjects, in the production of knowledge. While positivist, mainstream methodologies encourage research *on* or *about* people, an alternative approach encourages research *with* people. Through our participatory action methodology I was able to speak in solidarity with the women — for as a woman in this society I too have experienced oppression.

Canadian academics Sandra Kirby and Kate McKenna

provide strategies for an alternative approach to social research in their book *Methods from the Margins*. They define "the margins" as the context in which those who suffer injustice, inequality and exploitation live their lives.[8] They argue that many people, especially women, find themselves on the margins not only in terms of inequality in the distribution of material resources but also in terms of knowledge production, so that the views of a small group of people — usually economically privileged white males — are presented as "the truth." Focusing on the world from the perspective of those in the margins allows us to see the world differently and, in many ways, more authentically. And doing participatory action research allows us to create knowledge that is useful to those in the margins because it is knowledge that promotes social change.[9]

Participatory methodologies use qualitative rather than quantitative methods. Qualitative methods — in-depth interviews, for example — help researchers to explore, in rich and meaningful ways, complex social relations such as incest in Catholic families. Although qualitative research is criticized because it has limited generalizability beyond the research group to the wider population, qualitative methodologies can explain more adequately than quantitative methodologies the nuances and complexities of the social world.[10] In other words, what qualitative studies lose in breadth, they often gain in depth.

To say a study has limited generalizability is not to say it has no generalizability, however. A case study analysis allows for a special kind of generalization, *analytic generalization,* and differs from a sampling method that facilitates the more commonly recognized form of generalization, *statistical generalization.* Analytic generalization occurs when a previously developed theory about a social phenomenon is supported by one or more of the case studies. If two or more of the case studies support the theory, replication can be claimed, thereby strengthening the generalizability of the theory. In other words, analytic generalization uses a previously developed theory as a template with which to compare the empirical results of the case studies. Therefore, the development of a rich, theoretical framework, which states the conditions under which a phenomenon is likely to be found, is a necessary first step when using a case study approach. Statistical generalization, on the other hand, occurs in quantitative methodologies, such as surveys, in which researchers use preset formulas to determine, depending on the size of a sample and its internal variation, the confidence with which a generalization can be made to a wider population.[11]

Our participatory action methodology used a *case study* approach. The eight Catholic families as described from the standpoint of these incest survivors represent multiple case studies of Catholic family culture. My goal was to set out a theoretical framework (see Chapter 2) that would enable us to explore the complexities of incest in these eight families. If my theory about incest in Catholic families was generalizable to the case studies, I would be able to cite excerpts from the women's lives to help us chart fault lines between Catholic family life as it was *idealized* during the 1940s to the 1980s and everyday/everynight[12] Catholic family life as it was *actually experienced* during those decades.

Our methodology was not without its difficulties and limitations. It required a great deal of time and mutual commitment on my part and on the part of the participants. Patricia Maguire also suggests that it is often a challenge for the researcher to relinquish unilateral control over the research process.[13] In the case of our participatory action methodology, although it was difficult at times to do so, I felt it was especially important for me to relinquish unilateral control: as incest survivors, these women have histories that include a painful *loss* of control over their own lives and I wanted them to feel empowered as a result of participating in the study.

THE RESEARCH DESIGN

I designed the research process to allow us, over time, to build our knowledge about incest and Catholic family culture. I used three different methods in my research design: individual interviews, focus group interviews and textual analysis of official Catholic texts on marriage, family life and sexuality. Combined, these methods allowed us to explore these eight Catholic families as case studies of Catholic family culture.

I scheduled two sets of individual interviews, several months apart. The individual interviews were a rich source of information about the women's lives and experiences. As a way of helping the participants to feel in control of the process I met with them in their own homes or, when it suited them, at the local women's centre. One initial interview was held in the office of the participant's counsellor where she was accustomed to discussing her history of incest. I used open-ended questions and invited the women to reflect on aspects of their histories as incest survivors. During the set of follow-up interviews I asked additional questions based on the first set of interviews (see Appendices II and III).[14] I attempted to model my interviews on a true dialogue rather than an interrogation[15] by talking about my experiences as a Catholic and a feminist. I was glad to hear Maya say:

> The fact that you're a feminist and a Catholic helped me feel comfortable because I'm also a feminist and a Catholic. In a way it sort of put us on a footing where I

felt we had a mutual understanding. I felt that you knew where I was coming from for the most part and I felt I had a sense of where you were coming from. I'm trying to imagine being interviewed by a non-feminist or a non-Catholic — it would've been quite a different experience. I think it would be harder to feel that feeling of the two-way street. I mean, especially being a Catholic, it sort of puts you in the group with the participants, not just like some scientist from outside looking in.

My standpoint as a feminist helped Jackie to feel at ease:

I could be completely open and honest and not worry about what you were going to think about what I was telling you. I didn't have to choose my words. I knew you weren't going to judge me. If you'd been a non-feminist coming in and doing something like this I would've felt like I was going to be sort of scrutinized for what I was saying.

Mary said something similar:

I don't think anyone other than a feminist would do this kind of work. If they were doing it they'd probably be doing it from a perspective I wouldn't be very comfortable with — I'd feel like they were exploiting. I guess the feminist process helps you get through this in a way that someone else would do it as a business deal. Like being a book author, if that had started out being your number one objective, I doubt any of us would have felt comfortable with that.

At two points in the research process I held focus group[16] interviews — the first in August of 1994 (see Appendix IV), the second in March of 1995 (see Appendix V). In our case, the focus group interviews were similar in style to a feminist consciousness-raising or support group. We sat together with our chairs formed into a circle. I posed questions and loosely guided the discussion.[17] I was confident that group interviews would help us to uncover information that wouldn't have surfaced through individual interviews alone. Indeed, the women told me that hearing the views of the other participants encouraged them to think in new ways. Faye told me:

> I found the group interviews really interesting because you had other people talking about the Catholic context and that kind of triggered different ideas. Having the study spread out really helped, too. Between the first interview and the group interviews and so on I was able to do more thinking. So I thought it was a very good process — rather than just having one interview and leaving it you really gave us time to think and make connections.

Elizabeth said the collective storytelling helped her to synthesize her own experience:

> I think the group interview opened up a new area of having to look at things. There was a sense of not being alone in it. That's what the group does — the group helped a lot to be able to put this thing together, to kind of synthesize.

Before the group interviews I provided each participant with both the transcript of her most recent individual interview and the most recent research report. By providing the participants with their own transcripts as well as the research reports, I was able to keep them informed about ways the other participants were thinking about the questions and issues. The individual and group interviews created important opportunities for us to build our knowledge about incest and Catholic family culture in a communal way. Mary pointed out that the periods of time in between the interviews were crucial to her ability to synthesize and make connections:

I needed that time and I didn't even know that I needed it! At first I would have wanted to get it all over with in one day — over with and I'd never have wanted to see you or it again in that context. But it was good that it was structured this way [over several months]. I've changed a lot since the first interview — it's just incredible. The Pope's not doing a process, but we are. I don't think [members of the Catholic hierarchy] do come through a process. If they did they'd be coming from a more informed place.

The third component in my research design was the interplay between my reading of several official Catholic texts on marriage, family life and sexuality and my reading of the interviews. After the first set of interviews, when I realized I was dealing with two distinct sub-groups within the participant group (representing pre–Vatican II and post–Vatican II Catholicism respectively), I decided to look at some pre–Vatican II documents in addition to Pope John Paul II's 1981 apostolic exhortation on marriage and the family. I read Pope Leo XIII's 1880 encyclical on marriage, Arcanum Divinae Sapientiae, and Pope Pius XI's 1930 encyclical on marriage, Casti Connubii, as well as the influential handbook on marriage from the 1950s, Rev. George A. Kelly's *Catholic Marriage Manual*.[18] Together with the participants, I used these texts to help track the fault lines in the women's experiences. The interviews highlighted the Catholic texts as representative of a patriarchal, ideological vision of marriage and family life — the topic I explore in detail in Chapters 6, 7 and 8.

The Women's Experiences of the Research Process

I suggested earlier in this chapter that one goal of a participatory action methodology is to build solidarity between the researcher and participants. I therefore attempted to enter the research process as a sister collaborator and tried to promote a sense that we were learning together — no one had a monopoly on "the truth." The women told me they appreciated the care I took to create opportunities for feedback and dialogue within the research group. During the final set of interviews, when I asked the participants to reflect on the research process, Faye told me she felt empowered as a result of participating:

> I like the way you saw it as a collaborative enterprise, where we were really involved and able to give feedback and where you obviously took a lot of time, you know, to think about the confidentiality and how to set that up and reassure us. You were doing this as a researcher but there was a solidarity there as a researcher. We weren't just people you were examining in an objective way. I think it's much more humane than the old way of keeping research objective and non-involved. I found the whole [process] very helpful. Putting incest in a cultural context was good too — not just looking at the inner psychological stuff but how incest happens in a particular culture.

Maya was appreciative of the care and thought that went into the research process:

> The main thing that comes to mind for me is that the way you did things really communicates the respect you have for the participants — the care that was taken, you know, to ensure confidentiality, to welcome input, to be supportive in your comments, and the openness of your approach — it all showed respect. Speaking for myself, it made me feel not like the object of an interview so much as, I don't know, someone participating in a discussion. I felt like I was more than just a source of information. And I felt that

you weren't just here to gather material for this book, you also wanted to facilitate learning and to help me as much as to help your project.

Others felt the process helped them make links between Catholicism and their history of incest. Mary, for instance, said that she had never previously given thought to the significance of her Catholic history, yet when I interviewed her she was able to give many richly detailed accounts of ways in which Catholicism played a role in the incest:

> I don't think I ever thought about all this stuff from a Catholic perspective until I talked with you. Catholic is all I've ever known — I wouldn't know any other way to think. I'd never analyzed it much from the perspective you're looking at it so, for me, it's been a privilege to take part in the process.

Mary was also enthusiastic about being part of a study that may bring about social change:

> I'm really looking forward to seeing your book, even if I don't agree with some of it, that'll be fine. I can handle that. Having read some of your work I just feel it's going to go somewhere. It's going to be part of change. It's not going to be something that'll collect dust. We will be more empowered by writings like this and someone's got to do it. I'm too busy surviving. If I was only in your youthful shoes I think I would be doing similar work. I can't be the pioneer so you're doing it for us. And I think it's pretty exciting.

The women's experiences positively reflect several aspects of a successful participatory action methodology. The women felt empowered by their role in the research process and felt there was a sense of solidarity among us — a solidarity grounded in our common bond as Catholic (or ex-Catholic) women who are striving to bring about greater sexual justice in the world. The participants felt they gained insight into their own life histories by listening to the experiences of others and were glad to "get this topic more out in the open" — in other words, to participate in research that will help to end the cycle of violence in families.

A great deal of caring work went into building our feminist participatory action methodology in all its stages — from the initial interviews to securing final approval from each participant for the completed book manuscript. This caring work allowed me to develop rich and rewarding relationships with the participants, and, in turn, to act as a catalyst in fostering relationships among the participants themselves. This kind of caring work is largely invisible and is certainly undervalued in mainstream academic circles. Yet it is work that deserves to be recognized and encouraged. My work, and my own life, have been enhanced by my connection and sense of responsibility to these eight women.

To understand the teachings of the Catholic church as *ideology*, it is necessary to provide for readers the theoretical framework that gave shape to our feminist critique of Catholic family culture. In Chapter 2, therefore, I outline the principles of a socialist feminist critique of the family. I also describe the principles of feminist standpoint theory and conclude the chapter by demonstrating some links between the theory and the women's everyday/everynight experiences in Catholic families.

Chapter 2

The Standpoint of Catholic Incest Survivors: Developing a Theoretical Framework

Point of Theoretical Departure

THE COMPLEXITIES of women's oppression defy simple explanation. Since the second wave of feminism in the 1960s and 1970s, various theories have developed to explain women's oppression and articulate a vision of a more just society — liberal feminism (focusing on equal opportunities for women), radical feminism (focusing on women's sexual oppression within patriarchy) and socialist feminism (focusing on the complex interplay between women's sexual and economic oppression within patriarchy), to name a few.[1] Not all feminist theorists and activists attach themselves to such labels, and, even when they do, the lines between theories are often blurred. Nevertheless, feminist theorizing has been and continues to be an indispensable part of the movement for women's liberation and empowerment.

Between 1993 and 1997, as I conducted research with the eight participants and wrote this book, I refined and clarified my grounding in socialist feminism, what Alison Jaggar calls "the most convincing promise of constructing an adequate theory and practice for women's liberation."[2] I worked from the standpoint of these eight incest survivors and together we produced a critique of *Catholic ideology*. In doing so, we explored an important dimension of social justice — *sexual* justice. As we talked about and reflected on their struggles as incest survivors, these eight Catholic families became for me the "site" of my *feminist praxis* — the dynamic interplay between feminist theory and practice.

The writings of several feminist theorists became "strands" in a "web" of theory that gave shape to my analysis of these eight Catholic families. The theorists include Canadian sociologist Dorothy E. Smith; philosopher of science Sandra Harding; political philosopher Alison M. Jaggar; social theorists Nancy Hartsock and Gillian Walker; poet, author and feminist theorist Adrienne Rich; and feminist theologian Carter Heyward. As theorists, they have a number of things in common. First, their views are compatible with, if not explicitly identified with, socialist feminism. This means they are each concerned with the complex relationship between women's economic and sexual oppression within capitalist patriarchy. For socialist feminists, women's activity in the so-called private sphere — in other words, women's everyday/everynight lives in families — is a primary locus of theorizing. Therefore, my web of feminist theory was well suited to an exploration of Catholic families. In the first section of this chapter I draw on several of these theorists to explain socialist feminism in more detail.

Second, these theorists share a belief, whether implicitly or explicitly, that women's lives and struggles (within capitalist patriarchy on a macro level, within families on a micro level) create a *critical standpoint* on society. This standpoint reveals that social relations are oppressive for those outside the dominant group — that is, economically privileged white males.[3] While I acknowledge the influence of several theorists who have adopted feminist standpoint arguments, I situate my overall study within the emerging sociological tradition inspired by Canadian sociologist Dorothy E. Smith.[4] I explain feminist standpoint theory in the section following my discussion of socialist feminism.

A third commonality among the theorists is their critique of a conservative world-view — a view epitomized by official Catholic teachings on marriage and "the family." Conservatives support differential treatment of women and men on the basis that women are by "nature" or "biology" better adapted than men to perform the roles traditionally assigned to them — tasks related to the care of children and households.[5] In the final section of this chapter I explore Catholic ideology as a particular form of patriarchal ideology by contrasting official Catholic texts (that is, *idealized* Catholic family life) with brief accounts of women's everyday/everynight lives in Catholic families (that is, *actual* Catholic family life from the standpoint of women).

SOCIALIST FEMINISM

Socialist feminism is a composite of Marxist and radical feminism. In its simplest formulation, a Marxist analysis focuses on the economic relationships between human beings within a capitalist society. Marxists have long seen the nuclear family as a cornerstone of capitalism.[6] In turn, feminists in the Marxist tradition came to identify women's economic dependence on men within nuclear families as central to the maintenance of both capitalism and women's oppression. Marxists do not argue that women's oppression was created by capitalism but that the advent of capitalism intensified the degradation of women by allocating to them the socially necessary but unprofitable tasks in the private sphere, such as food preparation, domestic labour and the care of children.[7] Thus, for Marxist feminists, women's liberation requires that the economic functions performed by women in families be undertaken by the state (for example, in the form of publicly funded day care programs). Marxist feminists also argue that women should be paid a wage for domestic work.[8]

Radical feminism is grounded primarily in the sexual politics of lesbian feminists.[9] Its proponents view the *institution of compulsory heterosexuality* — exemplified by a lifelong, monogamous marriage in which a woman is economically dependent on her husband — as the cornerstone of women's oppression.[10] Adrienne Rich views the institution of compulsory heterosexuality as the common thread running through patriarchal ideology. She argues that women, even before capitalist patriarchy, have been forced into lifelong, monogamous marriages in order to survive economically and to maintain a level of respectability for themselves and their children. She writes:

> Whatever its origins, when we look hard and clearly at the extent and elaboration of measures designed to keep women within a male sexual purlieu, it becomes an inescapable question whether the issue we have to address as feminists is, not simple "gender inequality," nor the domination of culture by males, nor mere "taboos against homosexuality," but the enforcement of heterosexuality for women as a means of assuring male right of physical, economical and emotional access ... The failure to examine heterosexuality as an institution is like failing to admit that the economic system called capitalism or the caste system of racism is maintained by a variety of forces."[11]

Socialist feminists, then, combine the best of *Marxist* critiques of the family and *radical* feminist critiques of the family by emphasizing not only the significance of women's economic powerlessness relative to men but also the complex cluster of practices that enforce the institution of compulsory heterosexuality. In other words, socialist feminists advocate a theoretical position that gives primacy neither to the analysis of women's economic oppression within capitalism nor to the analysis of women's sexual oppression within patriarchy — capitalism and patriarchy are so intertwined that, in order to end one, we must work to end both.

By merging the views of Marxist and radical feminists, socialist feminists reconceptualize the issues presented by radical feminists — those related to sexuality, childbearing and childrearing, for example — by looking at them in economic terms. Socialist feminists also examine sexuality and economics in deliberately *historical* ways.[12] In other words, by borrowing from Marxism the historical materialist method, they attempt to show that gender and sexual relations are neither fixed nor biologically determined. Rather, gender and sexual relations change over time in response to concrete and tangible conditions (such as women's economic status and practices that enforce heterosexuality).

An important dimension of the institution of compulsory heterosexuality is a gendered division of labour,[13] and a primary objective for socialist feminists is to eliminate the gendered division of labour within families.[14] An end to the gendered division of labour would irrevocably alter marriage and family life as we know them. A socialist feminist formula for ending women's oppression therefore requires a dual focus: an end to women's economic dependence on men in families and an end to the institution of compulsory heterosexuality.

FEMINIST STANDPOINT THEORY:
AN EPISTEMOLOGY ROOTED IN SOCIALIST FEMINISM

> Like the lives of proletarians according to Marxian theory, women's lives make available a particular and privileged vantage point on male supremacy, a vantage point which can ground a powerful critique of the phallocratic institutions and ideology which constitute the capitalist form of patriarchy.[15]

Feminist standpoint theory is an epistemology that has emerged from the socialist feminist tradition. Among its proponents are Nancy Hartsock, Sandra Harding and Dorothy E. Smith. While each standpoint theorist has contributed to this emerging epistemology in unique ways, the main similarity among them is the shared assumption that women's everyday/everynight lives can generate a much-needed critique of dominant, male-centred claims about the social world. A feminist standpoint is constituted out of the epistemic advantage — recall *episteme* as the Greek word for knowledge — afforded by women's *struggle against oppression*. And, as Nancy Hartsock explains, this standpoint is grounded in women's "real, material activity" within capitalist patriarchy:

> An analysis which begins from the sexual division of labour — understood not as taboo, but as the real, material activity of concrete human beings — could form the basis for an analysis of the real structures of women's oppression …Women's lives, like men's, are structured by social relations which manifest the experience of the dominant gender and class. The ability to go beneath the surface of appearances to reveal the real but concealed social relations requires both theoretical and political activity.[16]

For feminist standpoint theorists, research that begins from women's standpoint within capitalist patriarchy can produce knowledge about the social world that counters the hegemony of patriarchal ideology.

Sandra Harding and Dorothy E. Smith were especially influential as I wove feminist standpoint arguments into my theoretical web. Sandra Harding was influential because she has not only developed her own version of feminist standpoint theory but has also helped to consolidate the work of several socialist feminists (including Hartsock and Smith) who have generated, to a large extent independently of one another, feminist standpoint arguments. I was also influenced by the powerful standpoint argument Dorothy Smith has developed in her feminist sociology: that the everyday/ everynight standpoint of those who are marginalized by the dominant order can expose as *ideology* what the dominant gender and class call *knowledge* about the social world. In the sections below I elaborate on both Harding and Smith's versions of standpoint theory and show how they guided my critique of Catholic families from the standpoint of incest survivors.

Sandra Harding: Consolidating the Contributions of Standpoint Theorists

Sandra Harding, a feminist philosopher of science,[17] argues that women's lives, by "virtue" of their struggles against oppression in a capitalist, patriarchal culture, are "valuable as beginning points for scientific and scholarly projects."[18] The notion of women's "standpoint" is derived from Hegel's master-slave dialectic, later borrowed by Marx to establish the proletarian standpoint. The crucial component is the notion that the condition of oppression gives oppressed persons epistemic privilege. In other words, oppressed and marginalized people can "see" and "know" in ways their oppressors cannot because they have fewer interests in maintaining the status quo.[19] Harding argues that women have less to lose by distancing themselves from dominant social relations; thus, perspectives from their lives can more easily generate fresh and critical analyses.[20] Nancy Hartsock suggests there are some groups from whose perspectives, *however well-intentioned members of these groups may be,* the real relations between human beings are not visible.[21]

Harding cautions, however, that standpoint theorists do not advocate beginning our research simply from women's *experiences.* This may lead us to the faulty, male-centred conclusions of traditional research, for women too hold sexist, classist and racist beliefs. Rather, "knowledge emerges for the oppressed through the struggles that they wage against their oppressors ... [A] feminist standpoint is not something that anyone can have simply by claiming it. It is an achievement."[22] Standpoint theorists remind us that starting thought from women's lives is not the same as saying that our own lives (if we are women) are the best places to begin our research. Standpoint theory argues *against* the idea that all social situations provide equally useful resources for learning about the world.[23] Simply put, the positions of the most marginalized are the best places from which to generate questions and criticisms about the social world. Furthermore, a standpoint theorist does not claim that her position is the best one simply because she is a woman. For example, a black lesbian woman is in a better position than a white heterosexual woman to describe the character of racism and heterosexism. By extension, "expert" assessments of incest are likely to be less accurate than those grounded in the actual experiences of incest survivors.

From the standpoint of incest survivors who have struggled against their oppression we can come to see incest as a profoundly oppressive practice within our capitalist, patriarchal culture. The standpoint of perpetrators would tell a different story altogether. In relation to my study, the *survivors,* not the *perpetrators,* of sexual oppression in Catholic families can be expected to provide a sound critique of sexual oppression in Catholic families because the survivors have fewer interests in maintaining patriarchal family relations.

Harding reminds us, however, that not all women are willing to struggle against patriarchal, capitalist oppression. "Women have less to lose, but not nothing to lose; gaining a feminist consciousness is a painful process for many women."[24] In the case of incest, not all incest survivors have an unequivocal interest in knowing about their abuse. Years of repressed memories among many survivors attest to the fact that not remembering abuse is often the safest way for survivors to navigate through their lives. (As Mary told me, "You can't live with the abuser and still keep the memory. Putting the memory aside you can live with them day to day and not go insane.") However, those incest survivors who have acknowledged their abuse and struggled against the dominant order that allowed them to be abused are in the best position to explain and ask critical questions about that dominant order.

DOROTHY E. SMITH: FEMINIST SOCIOLOGY FROM THE STANDPOINT OF WOMEN

Dorothy E. Smith's work was a special inspiration to me as I explored Catholic family culture from the standpoint of women. I took up the invitation[25] to use her concepts and techniques of analysis. Although I have never been taught by

Dorothy Smith, I know many who have and their enthusiasm for her work was infectious. In the foreword to a recent collection of essays by scholars who adopt Smith's approach, the author writes of Dorothy Smith: "She was always ahead of us, like a magnetic force, pulling us, rather than pushing us, to grasp 'how things actually work' ... Dorothy Smith's pedagogy was invigorating as it brought us safely out of theory, and from the safety of theorizing, to how the everyday world worked, as a matter that any of us could investigate."[26]

For Smith, a feminist sociology must begin with the everyday/everynight struggles of women who function as "outsiders within" the dominant ruling relations. In *The Conceptual Practices of Power* Smith defines the relations of ruling as "something more general than the notion of government as political organization. I refer rather to that total complex of activities, differentiated in many spheres, by which our kind of society is ruled, managed and administered."[27] For Smith, a socialist feminist, those who "rule, manage and administer" within capitalist patriarchy are economically privileged men. It is from women's standpoint that we see how ruling relations permeate all aspects of our social, economic and political lives.[28]

Ruling ideology creates a disjuncture, or "line of fault," because what women *actually* do within the dominant order is not always what it is in our *interest* to do. The line of fault becomes visible when women realize that the categories defined by men are "a forced set of categories into which we must stuff the awkward and resistant actualities of our worlds."[29] Smith explains:

> In the disclosures and discoveries of the women's movement, women's experience breaks away along [a] line of fault. It makes thus observable an apparatus of social controls in part ideological, in the sense of being images and symbols, and in part an organization of specialized practices.[30]

Throughout this book I use the terms "ideology" and "Catholic ideology." In doing so, I draw heavily on Smith's understanding of ideology, which is rooted in Marx and Engels's use of the term. Smith defines it as

> those ideas and images through which the class that rules the society by virtue of its domination of the means of production orders, organizes and sanctions the social relations that sustain its domination ... [T]he concept of ideology ... directs us to examine who produces what for whom ... [and] where the social forms of consciousness come from.[31]

Smith has adopted Marx and Engels's definition to explain the fault lines created in women's lives by ideological practices. These practices, organized by men in order to sustain their domination over women, *alienate* women from our own experience by compelling us "to think [our] world in the concepts and terms in which men think theirs."[32] Smith explains alienation in this way: "The simplest formulation of alienation posits a relation between the work individuals do and an external order oppressing them in which their work contributes to the strength of the order that oppresses them."[33] Women's alienation, as long as it remains unidentified and unchallenged, plays a pivotal role in maintaining ruling relations. Women (and many other marginalized groups such as lesbian women and gay men, aboriginal peoples and women and men of colour), then, are not only excluded from the making of culture and intellectual discourse, but the activities they perform within the dominant order often contribute to their own oppression. The central motivation behind the women's movement, then, is the desire to change societal institutions that alienate women from their experience,[34] including, among others, the media, our educational systems and patriarchal religious institutions such as the Catholic church.

In Gillian Walker's study of the battered women's movement in Canada, *Family Violence and the Women's Movement: The Conceptual Politics of Struggle,* the author helps us to understand Dorothy Smith's conceptual framework. Walker summarizes:

> Society as we know it is not random but organized, ordered, and governed, with varying degrees of efficiency perhaps, but nonetheless structured ... Under such a regime, as opposed to overtly totalitarian ones, we are not ruled on a day-to-day basis by terror but ideological procedures — ways of thinking, understanding and acting — that enlist us in our own ordering. Ideological procedures are a feature of the way our society is governed. They form part of the work of a ruling apparatus comprising a complex of relations, including the state, the managerial and administrative processes, education, the professions, the media, and so on, that organize and control contemporary capitalist society.[35]

At the same time, Walker is concerned that we do "a disservice to [ourselves] as women and to our understanding of the structuring, ordering, and ruling of society ... to regard ourselves as having been merely passive victims of historical processes controlled by a conspiracy of men."[36] Like Smith, she emphasizes that women have actively struggled, and continue to do so, against ideological practices. Through these struggles women make visible the points of disjuncture, the fault lines, in their lives. Furthermore, as a historical materialist, Smith emphasizes that the fault lines in women's experience become most clearly visible when historical and material conditions — a woman's new-found economic independence, for example — empower us to challenge ideological practices. Maya's story is a case in point: "It wasn't that I forgot the memories [of the incest] but I kind of ignored them for a long time. The first time I really started to think about the incest was when I moved away from home. I was in a safe place, earning my own money and I didn't have to play nicey-nicey anymore — pretending that nothing had happened."

CATHOLIC IDEOLOGY

Institutional religion plays an important role (more or less strongly given a variety of historical and social considerations)[37] in the way societies as a whole are ruled and organized. The development of capitalist patriarchy in western society has been shaped in important ways by Christianity. Some historians and theologians argue that the history of western culture and the history of Christianity are so closely linked as to be indistinguishable.[38] Clearly, Catholic theology and practices, both historically and in the present, uphold a patriarchal, conservative world-view. Recalling the definition of conservatism, we are reminded that religious conservatives tend to view as natural and divinely ordained women's responsibility for the unpaid care of children and domestic labour in households. Catholic ideology (as opposed to "mere" secular forms of patriarchal ideology) is especially difficult to challenge because it is grounded in a theological tradition that equates conservativism with "God's plan" for the world. In Catholic families, then, men's experience of power is grounded in and reinforced both by Catholic ideological practices and society's larger set of ideological practices. Catholic ideology might be thought of as just one "finger" among the many hands that create and organize patriarchal relations in society. For

Catholics, those who create and organize patriarchal relations include the Pope, the hierarchy of clergy and male theologians, *but most pervasively,* husbands, fathers and other male relatives into whose hands the church has delivered a "natural" and "divinely ordained" power.

As I developed my critique of Catholic ideology, the analysis of Carter Heyward, a lesbian feminist theologian, was highly influential. In her book *Touching Our Strength: The Erotic as Power and the Love of God,* Heyward examines structural sexism and heterosexism in Christian theology and practices, especially as they relate to women's sexual and economic oppression. For Heyward, sexual justice requires a revolutionary revaluation of women and sexuality, one that works to transform heterosexist and patriarchal religious ideology. Through her work as a feminist liberation theologian she is committed to making connections between sexuality, spirituality, and the ongoing struggle for sexual justice.[39]

While Chapters 5 through 8 of this book are devoted to charting in more detail fault lines for women in Catholic families, I want to close this theoretical chapter by beginning to demonstrate what I mean by "identifying fault lines." What follows illustrates the contrast between aspects of official Catholic theology on the family and actual everyday/everynight experiences in Catholic families.

Catholic theology, for far longer than this century (the century with which I am primarily concerned in this book), has promoted lifelong, monogamous and heterosexual marriage as part of "God's plan" for the world. In 1880, Pope Leo XIII proclaimed that marriage is an institution "not received from men but implanted by nature," one that has "God for its author."[40] Fifty years later Pope Pius XI asked this rhetorical question: "How many and how important are the benefits which flow from the indissolubility of matrimony"?[41] In the same document he outlined the duties to which a proper Catholic wife and mother ought to devote herself: "the cares of children and family."[42] In 1958, the Reverend George A. Kelly's influential *Catholic Marriage Manual* instructed Catholics: "A husband's natural instinct in marriage is to be head ... Nothing like this is natural to the woman."[43] In 1981, long after Vatican II and the beginnings of second-wave feminism, Pope John Paul II continued to insist that "the true advancement of women requires that clear recognition be given to the value of their maternal and family role, by comparison with all other public roles" and that "society should create and develop conditions favouring [women's] work in the home."[44]

Constructing a feminist sociology of Catholic families from the standpoint of women incest survivors allows us to identify some fault lines for women and girls in traditional Catholic families. It would be wrong to suggest that as Elizabeth, Cherrie, Faye, Mary, Courage, Maya, Content and Jackie recounted their everyday/everynight experiences within the dominant Catholic family order, they described their Catholic families in wholly dark and negative terms. But while there were good aspects to the upbringing of each one of them, they were unable to describe their Catholic family environments as empowering. With them, I identified official Catholic *teachings* as Catholic *ideology* — ideas, images and practices through which the Catholic church organizes and sanctions social relations that sustain the domination of men over women and children. As I reflected on the Catholic texts and the interviews, and shared my thoughts with the participants, I suggested we think about Catholic ideology as having two sub-categories — "Catholic family ideology," which defines gender roles in families, and "Catholic sexual ideology," which defines the parameters for "morally appropriate" sexual relations.

Content, whose mother cared for twelve children, had this to say about her mother's enormous (unpaid) childcare and domestic responsibilities: "It would have been very difficult for Mom to leave, definitely very difficult. She had nowhere to go. And what would she do with all these kids? It definitely would have been impossible." Courage's mother, who depended on her husband economically, was in a similar situation. "Mom did leave Dad once. My dad always made good money and he'd send us money, plus she was getting social assistance, but it wasn't very much. The homes we lived in in Ontario were always nice and she wasn't used to living in a rat-trap apartment." On the indissolubility of Catholic marriage, Faye had this to say, "My parents hated one another but they stayed together through thick and thin." Mary's account of being pressured into her marriage when she became pregnant "out of wedlock" led to "some struggle of a marriage." Finally, Maya told me about the fault line in her "double life" — created in the effort to hide from her family that she is sexually active: "I wouldn't ever let people know that I have a lover and we're sexually active. I'm pretty good at acting like this good Catholic — because I feel that if my family knew they would really hate me."

Chapter 3

INCEST: DEFINITIONS, THEORIES, SOCIAL CONTEXT

DURING THE 1980s Canadian society witnessed a dramatic increase in awareness and reported cases of child sexual abuse.[1] As a society we have been forced to come to terms with rampant sexual abuse in many of our institutions, from "the family" as institution to many of our more formal institutions — churches, orphanages, day care facilities and residential schools, to name but a few. A mid-1980s national survey found that in a random sample of over 2,000 Canadian adults more than half of the women surveyed and about a third of the men had been forced into at least one unwanted sexual act — four-fifths of these occurring before adulthood.[2]

In order to understand this widespread abuse and how it applies to the eight women in my study, it is important to contextualize sexual abuse as a social phenomenon that is fundamentally rooted in patriarchy.[3] Incest, as I define it, is a particularly acute manifestation of child sexual abuse. Its long-term consequences are touched on in this chapter, and two non-feminist theories that attempt to explain incest are contrasted with a feminist analysis. By looking closely at the wider societal context in which incest occurs — notably the socio-economic realities of mothering — we gain a deeper understanding of this form of abuse.

Definitions of Child Sexual Abuse

Rix Rogers, appointed in the late 1980s as the special adviser on child sexual abuse to Canada's minister of health and welfare, reminds us that we are at a crucial time in history, a time when children's rights — especially their right to freedom from abuse — are recognized by the United Nations. He states that a "long-term and effective response to sexual abuse of children demands that we address deeply rooted contributing factors in our society. We must challenge patriarchal values that allow the more powerful to exploit the less powerful."[4] He defines sexual abuse as "the misuse of power by someone who is in authority over a child for the purposes of exploiting a child for sexual gratification. It includes incest, sexual molestation, sexual assault and the exploitation of the child for pornography or prostitution."[5] Similarly, Chris Bagley suggests that the

> sexual abuse of children takes many forms, and is certainly not confined to the intercourse defined by the incest statute. Sexual abuse can range from the sexualization of children for commercial purposes ... to the exploitation of children through pornography; to various kinds of sexual assault ranging from exposure and manual interference to the grossest forms of sexual assault.[6]

In the literature on child sexual abuse, the terms sexual abuse and incest are sometimes used interchangeably. For example, in *The Best Kept Secret: Sexual Abuse of Children,* Florence Rush examines marriage laws in the Hebrew and

Christian traditions to make links with present-day incest practices and reminds us that, historically, patriarchal owner-ship of women and children was not necessarily confined within families. Indeed, Judaic and Christian patriarchal cul-tures allowed men to violate the boundaries of women and children both within and beyond family contexts.[7] My defini-tion of incest is most strongly modelled on the one used by Annie Imbens and Ineke Jonker in *Christianity and Incest* and includes a continuum of acts and practices that violate the sex-ual boundaries of vulnerable (usually female) family members:

> When we use the word incest, we are not referring to vol-untary contact between adult family members (blood rela-tives) or sexual relations between children in a(n) (extended) family which occur with mutual consent. We use the word "incest" to refer to sexual abuse of children within the (extended) family. The term "sexual abuse within the (extended) family" refers to sexual contacts ini-tiated by adults (father, stepfather, uncle, grandfather, a friend of the family, older brother), in which the wishes and feelings of the child with whom the acts are commit-ted are not taken into account.[8]

Based on this definition, I assume that a family environ-ment in which incest occurs is "poisonous" for the vulnerable family members. A story from Maya's life illustrates the no-tion that incest can range from "mild" to "severe." While Maya's history of incest primarily involved her uncle, she told me that her father's "serious issues about sexuality" also helped to create a poisonous family environment:

> I remember Dad's reaction when we [my sisters and broth-ers and I] started dating. I didn't really start to date until I was nineteen. I remember that Dad was morbidly curious

about the details of my love-life. One time he asked my sister, "So, who's Maya sleeping with now?" And I wasn't even dating at the time! It was so absurd and I was very hurt by it. I felt it was a violation of my privacy and showed an unhealthy interest in my personal life. Since he didn't know what was going on he was imagining what he considered to be the worst scenario ... He's even been known to say, "If you weren't my daughter I'd be interested in you."

In a related way, I also assume that, as a form of family violence, incest exists alongside and often overlaps with other gender-based forms of violence — such as the battering of women in families — for each form of violence has roots in a culture that devalues women and (especially female) children, and fosters relations of dominance and subordination.

Incest is a particularly pernicious form of sexual abuse because it very often involves a betrayal of trust by someone on whom the child depends for survival. And the perpetrator is usually someone the child loves. On the other hand, sexual abuse between a child and a stranger doesn't, at least to the same extent, involve a betrayal of trust. Incest survivors who disclose to family members often encounter tremendous resistance — for the abuse is occurring in the very place the child expects to turn for protection. When abuse is disclosed, loyalties (especially for women who must respond as both mother to an abused child and partner to an abuser[9]) can become fiercely divided. Not surprisingly, incest families, whether the abuse is out in the open or not, are often filled with fear, hostility and instability.[10] An excerpt from Jackie's life story tells this tale:

Once I identified myself as a survivor I withdrew from my mother and I blamed her. I guess I held her responsible in a way. I felt she should have been able to stop it because as long as I could remember she knew my stepfather was always being mean to me. Not so much about the sexual abuse but she knew about the physical abuse. So I was hoping she'd clue in and say, "Okay, that's enough." In my mind I guess I hoped she would get rid of him and that type of thing. So I had a lot of misdirected anger towards her. I think at some level she knew that something was definitely wrong but I think she was scared herself — she didn't know what to do.

SEXUAL ABUSE AND INCEST:
LONG-TERM CONSEQUENCES

The long-term consequences of sexual abuse are now better understood than ever before. This is largely because women have undertaken research from a more compassionate and understanding place. Many have adopted a feminist standpoint approach to develop a sense of solidarity with survivors and by doing so have avoided the researcher/research subject hierarchy that typifies positivist research. Ellen Bass and Laura Davis's guide for survivors of sexual abuse, *The Courage to Heal,* is an example of a feminist standpoint approach. Bass and Davis stand alongside the survivors and choose not to remain politically neutral — they take a clear position against patriarchy.

None of the findings in studies looking at long-term consequences are very surprising. One study conservatively estimates that at least a quarter of child sexual abuse carries a legacy of serious long-term psychological harm to survivors.[11] The most serious long-term effects of child sexual abuse result from incest, especially if the abuse was violent, involved penetration and took place over long periods of time. Predictably, researchers have found that sexual abuse by a parent or step-parent involves the greatest betrayal and loss of trust for survivors. And incest survivors have significantly lower self-esteem, more sexualized attitudes and behaviours and poorer overall health than women who were not abused in childhood.[12]

All eight of the women I worked with in this study disclosed serious long-term harm resulting from their incest histories. Content told me the abuse robbed her of her ability to stand up for herself and to trust men in intimate relationships:

> I never told anybody because I thought, "Well, he isn't hurting me — physically anyway." Emotionally, ya, but you don't realize that till you're older. Then you're really screwed up ... When I was a kid, I could never say no to my brother if he wanted to come at me. And so when I was a child, at school, with teachers or whatever, if I got blamed for something I would never speak up and say I didn't do it. And when I was a teenager, because I didn't want guys to get close to me, I never really had boyfriends. The sexual abuse always scared me away from relationships. I thought that all guys wanted was sex. But maybe there would have been someone who did want to get to know me better and I scared him away. I'll never know that. Maybe I could have had a high school sweetheart kind of thing. I don't know. It makes me feel robbed and I wonder what my life would be like if the sexual abuse had never happened.

Intergenerational patterns of sexual abuse — abuse occurring from one generation to the next — are also very common.[13] Some survivors of abuse become perpetrators as adults and many survivors become mothers of survivors. Mary, who in childhood was raped repeatedly by her father, explained the generational patterns of abuse in her family:

> My father sexually abused me, he abused my daughter and God knows how many other children he abused. But knowing that my father had been sodomized himself umpteen times by his uncle sort of makes me understand things a little better. It helps you understand how people can get stuck in a certain place of wrongness — and yet be so correct at other times and have a family and be a good father overall.

The repression of sexual abuse memories, also called dissociation or "splitting," is known as the *sine qua non* of severe sexual abuse. Repressing the memories of abuse is a primary coping mechanism in the aftermath of incest trauma. Empirical research has helped us to take this phenomenon seriously. It usually involves an involuntary "separation" from one's body while the abuse is happening. After the abuse, a survivor will repress the memories as a way of maintaining a personal identity that excludes the experience of having been abused.[14] Several of the women in my study repressed their memories of incest; at least four of the women repressed the memories until well into adulthood. Faye recollected that the process of repressing the knowledge of abuse was like "splitting [her] mind in two":

> There was the good father, the one I trundled around after wherever he went, and there was the "bad man." He wasn't the "bad father" since I denied it was my father doing these things to me. It was the "bad man" who'd do things to me. And to my child's mind they were two different people. While it was actually happening, I would do this fantasy thing, go into the wallpaper. While it was happening it

wasn't happening. That's what makes you feel crazy. It's like splitting your mind in two.

Meanwhile, however, memories of abuse, although not conscious, are "stored" in a survivor's body and are likely to manifest themselves in one or more of the many long-term symptoms of child sexual abuse: depression, eating disorders, chemical addictions, inexplicable body pain — the list goes on.[15] Elizabeth, for example, remembers a time that her father abused her by fondling her breasts and ejaculating on her lower back. When she made the connection between the trauma and her physical pain, she exclaimed, "No wonder I have lower back pain today!" Mary related that her body responded when she began to remember her history of incest. As she recalled the abuse, she had bouts of asthma, an illness that had left her in adolescence at about the same time that the abuse ended with her father: "When I was working through the memories with my counsellor I was just floating. I was up there looking down at this child and then I realized that the child was me. And what am I having? I'm having an asthma attack, a friggin' asthma attack!"

Dissociating from the incest is a way for survivors to cope with irreconcilable realities. On one hand, survivors wish to view their families as supportive and loving; on the other hand, an experience of incest conveys a strong message that their family has failed them in a fundamental way. Viewed in this light, dissociation and repressed memories illustrate Smith's claim that ideological practices, such as incest, work to *alienate* women from their everyday/everynight experiences.[16]

In Defence of Patriarchy:
Two Theories Explaining Incest

Maternal collusion theory (or *"mother blaming"*) has been a popular way of explaining incest. The theory upholds a belief that a mother's failure to assume an "appropriate" wifely role forces the role onto her daughter. In 1972, Herbert Maisch published a study on incest that provides a case in point. He suggested that marital disharmony or a wife's absence from the home may create temptations for a father to sexually abuse his daughter:

> Disturbed contact before the [incest] act between the male partner and his wife, and a negative to openly hostile relationship on the part of the victim towards her mother, belong to the essential characteristics of that disharmony which is symptomatic of family disorganisation ... A wife who is seriously ill, confined to bed for a lengthy period, or perhaps even has to go to the hospital, a mother who is having a baby, the fact that the couple go to work at different times ... all [provide] opportunities which, under certain conditions, may give rise to situations of temptation [for the father].[17]

Mother blaming continues to be evident in recent studies. A 1993 study about mothers of incest survivors leaves no room to consider the broader socio-economic implications of mothering in contemporary society:

> Although fathers, stepfathers, and other male relatives are the perpetrators in nearly all incidents of incestuous sexual abuse, many researchers see mothers as important co-contributers. Some investigators ... have gone so far as to argue that mothers are "the real abuser" and actually "engineer the incestuous relationship." ... Despite this extreme

view, it seems important to differentiate between mothers who might actually conspire with the perpetrator in order to avoid sex, physical abuse, or obtain personal gain, those who simply fail to protect a child from the advances of a perpetrator, and those who make the child more vulnerable to sexual overtures from others as a result of inadequate parenting practices or poor parent-child relationships.[18]

In the last twenty years or so, feminist theorists have refuted analyses that blame mothers by looking at the wider social and economic contexts in which incest occurs. Researchers with the Child Abuse Studies Unit at England's University of North London write in defence of mothers:

> Mother blame needs to be placed in the context ... of mothers being held responsible for family well being, and particularly the expectation that women, and wives especially, service men physically, emotionally and sexually. Whilst systematically denied social power, women are held responsible for men's sexuality, men's violence and children's safety.[19]

In *Mothers of Incest Survivors: Another Side of the Story,* Janis Tyler Johnson explores the factors that can make it difficult for mothers of incest survivors to opt for the welfare of their daughters, especially if their own welfare depends on maintaining a relationship with their husbands.[20] In her study with six mothers of incest survivors, she found some interesting commonalities among them:

> [All of the] mothers shared the traditional world of women before they came into the research situation. They all began their marriages young (the average age was nineteen) ... They were all economically dependent upon their husbands and in some cases emotionally and socially dependent as

well. They all came from traditional families of origin where the models of male-female and husband-wife hierarchical relationships reinforced and supported their economic dependency. Mothers stayed home, and if they had ever worked, they returned to the home after marrying, and those who returned to work outside the home usually encountered a great deal of resistance from their husbands.[21]

She also found that these six mothers had experienced some form of abuse during their marriages and that all but one of the women were realistically afraid of their husbands. In other words, the incest occurred within a wider context of family violence.[22]

Feminists do not turn a blind eye to the fact that many mothers respond inadequately in the aftermath of incest. But instead of accusing mothers of collusion, pathology or inadequacy,[23] feminists view mothers' responses to incest in the context of profound and conflicting pressures placed on them within a patriarchal, capitalist society — a context I explore later in this chapter and in Chapter 7 of this book.

Another theory, which I call *pathology theory,* individualizes sexual abuse by looking to the individual perpetrator, or to an individual family, for the source of "pathology" or "dysfunction." According to this theory, the perpetrator is thought to be committing a deviant, antisocial act that most "normal," strong-willed people would not commit. The fact that most perpetrators are men and most victims are girls is not considered. The act is viewed as an isolated social event, and a problem that can be dealt with through individual measures — such as private therapy for the perpetrator.[24]

Feminists do not view incest as an isolated act between one individual and another. They see it as intimately connected to the complex cluster of social forces that promote

compulsory heterosexuality and eroticize female powerlessness and male aggression.[25] A feminist analysis suggests that,
while it is important to hold individual abusers accountable,
it may be too easy to blame individuals without viewing the
social context in which individuals are shaped and act. A feminist analysis, then, views incest and other forms of abuse as
*profoundly destructive and regrettable but nevertheless pre-
dictable* given the economic and political disparity between
women and men in contemporary society.

Inherent to pathology theory is a conservative bias that
tends to view the violent and ugly aspects of family life as
atypical deviations.[26] According to the theory, families that
deviate from a traditional family model are considered more
likely to foster abuse than families with a traditional structure. A feminist analysis of incest counters this theory and
puts forward evidence to suggest that a conservative family
structure can actually *foster* abuse. For instance, in *Sexual
Abuse in Christian Homes and Churches,* Carolyn Holderread
Heggen cites quantitative findings that conservative religios-
ity is the second most important predictor (next to the abuse
of alcohol or drugs) of incest:

> If you want to know which children are most likely to be
> sexually abused by their father, the second most significant
> clue is *whether or not the parents belong to a conservative re-
> ligious group with traditional role beliefs and rigid sexual at-
> titudes* [italics in the original].[27]

As early as 1978 Sandra Butler, in *Conspiracy of Silence: The
Trauma of Incest,* suspected this link: "Were it possible to provide a more realistic profile of a typical family in which incestuous abuse occurs, it would more likely be a middle-class
family composed of husband, wife and children living together in a nuclear situation."[28]

ATTENDING TO SOCIAL CONTEXT:
THE SOCIO-ECONOMIC REALITIES OF MOTHERING

As I suggest above, the gendered division of labour in society and within families provides a central context for understanding family violence. Despite women's contributions to the Canadian economy (estimates suggest that women's unpaid labour contributes 32 per cent to 59 per cent of the gross national product in Canada), women's domestic and reproductive labour is largely unpaid and undervalued.[29] Violence and poverty are linked to women's responsibility for the care of children since women's unpaid labour hinders their efforts to protect themselves and their children.

Violence against women in Canada is a widespread social problem. In 1993, almost half of Canadian women surveyed reported violence by men known to them. One in six married women reported domestic violence and of those more than one in ten felt that at some point their lives had been in danger.[30] The abuse of women in families causes profound physical and psychological damage and negatively affects children who witness violence. Men's control of financial resources in families sets up an imbalance of power between spouses, an imbalance that is intensified when violence enters the picture.[31] Simply put, then, economic dependence, and the threat of poverty for women in the event of a breakup, help to preserve family violence in its many forms.

In recent decades, Canadian trends in family demographics have been moving away from a traditional family structure[32] but in the wake of these changes has come an additional stress for mothers: poverty. Family trends in Canada point to increasing levels of poverty among families composed of single women with children. Between 1971 and 1986, the number of working poor women in Canada increased by 160.4 per cent.[33] Underlying the feminization of poverty is women's continued responsibility for child-rearing: women's resources are taxed as they bear the brunt of costs associated with raising children and attempt to work full time or further their education. In a patriarchal, capitalist society such as ours, in which women continue to be responsible for the care of children, women often end up poor when they take a stand against male violence. The implications are profound for the welfare and quality of life of women and the children they care for.[34]

Socialist feminists Michèle Barrett and Mary McIntosh argue that a restructuring of the gendered division of labour is a prerequisite for women's (and children's) empowerment and their ability to make authentic choices. To achieve these goals Barrett and McIntosh advocate structural economic changes in society — such as publicly funded day care programs and meaningful, full-time employment for women.[35] But the social supports that would permit a fundamental restructuring of the division of labour within Canadian households do not yet exist. The lack of a federally funded national day care program in Canada is a prime example. In a recent study on the gendered division of labour, Canadian sociologist Meg Luxton highlights women's economic dependence as a primary obstacle to challenging male power:

> Despite the obvious interest ... women have in redistributing domestic labour, and despite their motivating anger, there are numerous forces operating which make it difficult ... Because inequalities in the division of labour are based on male power, when women demand equalization they are challenging that power ... [E]conomic dependency makes it more difficult to challenge men in the household.[36]

Feminist research, then, suggests that we still have a long way to go to challenge a fundamental tenet of patriarchal ideology — the gendered division of labour that makes women responsible for the vast majority of reproductive and domestic labour. And feminist research on family violence suggests that we still have a long way to go in bringing about a necessary (albeit insufficient) condition for rooting out sexual violence in families — a radical change in women's socio-economic status within Canadian society. In the chapters to come, I examine the implications for incest survivors of Catholic family culture, which has helped to entrench a gendered division of labour within families and society as a whole.

Chapter 4

CATHOLIC IDEOLOGY AND INCEST: TRACING HISTORY, MAKING CONNECTIONS

The image of Father God, spawned in the human imagination and sustained as plausible by patriarchy, has in turn rendered service to this type of society by making its mechanisms for the oppression of women appear right and fitting. If God in "his" heaven is a father ruling "his" people, then it is the "nature" of things and according to divine plan and the order of the universe that society be male dominated.[1]   — Mary Daly

Father God to me, that whole image was a horrifying one, and one that I could never relate to very well. Which makes sense if you've been abused by your father — it can become a terrifying kind of image.   — Faye

Knowing that sex was such a loaded issue made it impossible. I felt it was impossible to go to my parents for help. I thought I would be punished and blamed.   — Maya

We've been burned at the stake in our way, anyone that's been burned sexually.   — Mary

WE DON'T have to look long at Catholicism to find evidence of patriarchy. Many feminist scholars (sociologists, historians and theologians, among others) have provided critiques of Catholic culture — its practices, teachings and beliefs — from the standpoint of women.[2] They have examined a broad range of women's experiences of oppression within the Catholic church, including (but not limited to) the persecution of women accused of witchcraft during the Middle Ages and various forms of domestic violence. Women's experiences of oppression expose many Catholic practices as *ideological practices* — practices that support an ideology of men's domination over women and children. Feminist scholars counter claims that the Catholic church has been the liberator of women[3] and that Catholic church history is a "luminous testimony to the dignity of women."[4] Rather, they suggest that the church's treatment of women has promoted women's (and by extension children's) vulnerability more often than — as various popes have suggested — women's emancipation, liberation and advancement.

In exploring Catholic ideology from the standpoint of women I use the terms Catholic *sexual* ideology and Catholic *family* ideology in order to link two complementary tenets of Catholic patriarchal ideology. Catholic sexual ideology refers to the Catholic teaching that sexuality is to be expressed *only* between heterosexual, monogamous spouses, whose bond is indissoluble and whose every act of sexual intercourse is open to the possibility of new life. Catholic family ideology refers to Catholic teachings that make women in families responsible for childcare and domestic labour. Over the centuries, Catholic sexual and family ideology has remained surprisingly consistent — and these tenets of Catholic ideology have shaped to an astonishing degree the practices that have allowed men to control women's fertility, limit women's autonomy and stifle the realization of women's intellectual potential. The voices of incest survivors help us make connections between Catholic ideology, as it developed historically, and Catholic family culture in the twentieth century.

SOME HISTORICAL ROOTS OF CATHOLIC IDEOLOGY[5]

Among Catholic ideology's most notable characteristics is its disparagement of women and sexuality — perhaps an unsurprising fact given that Catholic ideology is rooted in patriarchal theology. The development of Catholic theology has been influenced not only by the writings of early Christians but also by pagan and Judaic belief systems that were similarly patriarchal and sexually pessimistic. For instance, Catholic teachings about women and sexuality emanate from the Judaic creation myth that rendered Eve (and therefore all women) responsible for the fall of "man." This myth has played an important role in justifying the belief that women are morally inferior to men and therefore deserving of punishment and abuse.[6] Over time the strong influence of the Catholic church in the development of societies in Western Europe (especially during the medieval period) entrenched the disparagement of women and sexuality within those societies. In more recent centuries, the combined efforts of European colonialism and Catholic missionary activity helped to spread the disparagement of women and sexuality throughout western culture as a whole.

Two medieval philosophers,[7] Saint Augustine (354–430) and Saint Thomas Aquinas (1224–1274), were especially influential in the formation of Catholic theology, and, in turn, western culture. Augustine's and Aquinas's philosophical positions were guided by two traditions of Greek philosophy,

Platonism in Augustine's case and Aristotelianism in that of Aquinas. Platonism is characterized by a radically dualistic vision of the world and human nature. In this world-view, women are associated with material, earthly realities — nature, the body and sexuality — while men are associated with more lofty realities — God, the soul and intellectual pursuits. Augustine's writings therefore accentuated a disdain for material realities, especially sexuality, and idealized spiritual and intellectual values.[8] For example, Augustine believed sexual desire was evil and that married couples put the evil of sexual desire to good use *only* when each and every conjugal act served the purpose of procreation — sexual intercourse without this goal would "imply a surrender to lust."[9] Indeed, this belief permeated Catholic theology throughout the centuries. Only a Catholic who was pleasureless was without sin, as feminist theologian Uta Ranke-Heinemann points out:

> Saint Augustine, the greatest of all the Fathers of the Church, was the man responsible for welding Christianity and hostility to sexual pleasure into a systematic whole ... To speak of sexual hostility, therefore, is to speak of Augustine. He was the theological thinker who blazed a trail for the ensuing centuries — indeed, for the ensuing millennium. The history of the Christian sexual ethic was shaped by him. The binding nature of Augustine's pronouncements was accepted by the great theologians of the middle ages, notably Thomas Aquinas.[10]

Saint Thomas Aquinas, one of the most authoritative theologians in the history of Christianity, was influenced by the resurgent interest in Aristotelian philosophy in the thirteenth century. He incorporated into Catholic dogma many of Aristotle's beliefs, the most important one for women being the belief that women are misbegotten males.[11] To Catholicism's already prevalent disparagement of women and sexuality, Aquinas added the belief that women are fit only for child-bearing and ill-qualified for spiritual and intellectual pursuits. He wrote:

> I cannot see to what end woman was created as a helpmate for man if the generative purpose be excluded ... To what end is woman given to man, if not as an aid to the bearing of children? Perchance that they should till the soil together? If help had been needed to that end, a man would have been of more assistance to the man. The same may be said of consolation in solitude. How much more agreeable it is for life and conversation when two [male] friends dwell together than when man and woman cohabit.[12]

Theologians of that period also made overt proclamations about women's evil and cunning nature — a nature that, once again, rendered them deserving of punishment. Albertus Magnus, a prominent theologian and teacher of Thomas Aquinas, taught:

> Woman is a stranger to fidelity. Believe me, if you put your faith in her you will be disappointed. Believe an experienced teacher. Prudent husbands, therefore, apprise their wives of their plans and doings least of all. Woman is an imperfect man and possesses, compared to him, a defective and deficient nature. She is therefore insecure in herself. That which she herself cannot receive, she endeavors to obtain by means of mendacity and devilish tricks. In short, therefore, one must beware of every woman as one would of a poisonous serpent and the horned devil ... Woman is not more intelligent than man, properly speaking, but more cunning. Intelligence has a good ring, cunning an evil one. Thus, woman is cleverer, that is to say, more cunning, than man in evil and perverse dealings.[13]

To compensate for women's moral inferiority, Catholicism idealized Mary, the virgin mother of Jesus, and held her up as a model of redeemed womanhood. Mary, the obedient virgin, contrasted with Eve, the temptress. Thus Catholic sexual ideology came to idealize virginity and asexuality. While the Virgin Mary's paradoxical virginal and maternal status (achieved by divine intervention) is an impossible ideal for actual women to achieve, Catholic sexual ideology nevertheless upholds for women this contradictory ideal. Radical feminist theologian Mary Daly argues: "Catholicism has offered women compensatory and reflected glory through identification with Mary. [But t]he inimitability of the Virgin Mother model ... has left all women essentially identified with Eve."[14] And Ranke-Heinemann maintains that Catholic ideology's devotion to the Virgin Mary

> has become a kind of anti-Mariology in that it claims to emphasise a woman's greatness and dignity and paint them in glowing theological colours while crudely destroying all that constitutes feminine dignity in Mary the human being in particular and in all women in general ... Everything connected with female sexuality, all that betokens the natural generation and bearing of children, have been denied her ... She was thus transformed into a kind of sexless creature, a mere semblance of a wife and mother restricted to her role in the redemptive process.[15]

John Paul II's 1981 exhortation on marriage and the family suggests that Catholic ideology continues to idealize the Virgin Mary and to assume that women are in special need of redemption: "God ... manifests the dignity of women in the highest form possible, by assuming human flesh from the Virgin Mary, whom the church honours as the mother of God, calling her the new Eve and presenting her as the model of redeemed woman."[16] While this reference is brief and subtle, it seems that the myth of women's moral inferiority remains a tenet of late-twentieth-century Catholic ideology.

Some Catholic families in the late twentieth century still reward virginity and sexual purity. In Maya's family, for example, sexuality was denied and stifled — and her family's denial of sexuality made it next to impossible to tell anyone about the incest:

> I used to tell people I was asexual — like an amoeba. I would reproduce by spores or by budding! So, the family culture was denial of sexuality. When I finally did start dating [in my twenties] my relationships [with men] were always problematic. My mother modelled this type of asexuality for me. My mother upholds the basic Catholic family value of all the women in her family — that you shouldn't sleep with a man before you're married, because men are basically at the mercy of their hormones and you have to guard your virginity until you get married. So knowing that sex was such a loaded issue made it impossible. I felt it was impossible to go to my parents for help. I thought I would be punished and blamed.

Despite the inimitability of the Virgin Mary, Catholic women have been told to emulate her either by remaining virgins (for instance, by joining religious congregations) or by safely confining sexuality within a procreative marriage. Incest represents a profound breach of the Catholic teaching that sexuality must be expressed *only* between consecrated spouses. Thus incest survivors learn to identify themselves with Eve the temptress rather than Mary the virgin. While for some survivors the effects of the myth of women's inferiority may be subtle and covert, for others the effects are direct and unequivocal. In Faye's case, her father justified the incest by comparing them to Adam and Eve. Almost from infancy, and into her early teenage years, she was forced into acting like a consenting partner in the incest:

> I've been thinking about the Garden of Eden and what an important myth that is. It was in the Garden of Eden and it was Eve that tempted Adam and in a sense ruined the whole human race. So I think that's where a lot of our women's guilt comes from. My father had this kind of fantasy where we were both creatures in the Garden of Eden, both innocent children enjoying each other's bodies. The horror of it for me is that I felt I had to act like I wanted this just as much as he did and I hated him more for that. I got the idea that, of course, it was my fault, because, of course, it was Eve's fault.

The upshot of the myth of women's moral inferiority, along with an impossible ideal of sexual purity for women, has been the justification of women's punishment and abuse. Mary Daly states:

> Patriarchal religion adds to the problem [of women's oppression] by intensifying the process through which women internalize the consciousness of the oppressor. The males' judgment having been metamorphosed into God's judgment, it becomes the religious duty of women to accept the burden of guilt ... What is more, the process does not stop with religion's demanding that women internalize such images. It happens that those conditioned to see themselves as "bad" or "sick" in a real sense become such.[17]

In other words, through Catholic beliefs about women and sexuality, women come to believe that they are *in fact* morally inferior and deserving of punishment. Historically, the combined myths of women's moral inferiority and the special demand for women's sexual purity strengthened Catholic ideology — as long as women themselves believed they were deserving of punishment and abuse, the ideology was certain not to be challenged.

The myth of women's moral inferiority has justified horrific violations of women. During the medieval period the Catholic church led the persecution of women accused of witchcraft and sorcery. Women who displayed signs of autonomy (especially sexual autonomy) were targeted, as were women who practiced midwifery and the healing arts. Fundamentally, these women were persecuted because they posed a threat to the patriarchal order. The witch hunts were justified on the basis of Catholic church claims about woman's "naturally demonic nature" and her inability to control her lustful disposition due to both her inferior moral nature and her greater corruption by sin.[18]

Yet the belief that women are deserving of punishment in matters regarding sexuality has not been lost in history. The Catholic family culture described by the participants in my study suggests that this belief is alive and well. In one of her interviews, Mary told me that what she endured connects her to all women who were persecuted by the church in earlier centuries:

> You lived to be a saint [when I was young] — that was your aim. You wouldn't say that out loud, that you wanted to be a saint, but that *was* our aim. That's why we had to be so pure. Pure vessels. We've been burned at the stake in our way, anyone that's been burned sexually. Like myself, I sometimes feel that I've been so damaged that I've almost gone through some kind of maintenance process through most of my life, but now the Band-Aid's off and I don't even need a Band-Aid any more. I guess I feel like the

warrior stage has come, like I am Joan of Arc — I've been burnt but I've resurrected.

Mary's history of incest deeply affected her self-esteem — for a "good Catholic girl" was expected to be sexually pure. She described a rare moment of relief during her childhood that contrasted with her usual feelings of unworthiness:

> I remember once being in a concert at school. My mother prepared me for it and I was to sing "Star of the East." I got to solo and I had to hold a star and wear this long dress. I looked so angelic — I had feelings of being really pure. I felt wonderful that night even though while I was practicing for it with my mother I didn't feel great — we always thought of my mother as like Mary, the pure part of the family. In hindsight I can see what was probably going on. I was only ten or eleven and my abuse was still happening. This was me stepping outside of myself. This was the *pure* me.

Faye's history of incest led to a similarly profound feeling of unworthiness. Feeling certain that she was "beyond redemption," she rejected the church altogether:

> I really felt irredeemable. Whatever was happening to me was so bad that I was unsaveable, irredeemable. I still remember that feeling. I didn't really know what it was coming from because I repressed a lot of [the abuse]. But I remember feeling that feeling — having done something so bad that it was irredeemable. So when I left the convent school I left the church. I think, at base, I felt that I was too bad to ever be loved by God.

In addition to challenging the myths of women's moral inferiority and women's special need for redemption, feminist scholars challenge Catholic family ideology's belief that "the Catholic family" — characterized by a monogamous, lifelong sexual bond between spouses, a procreative sexual ethic and a division of labour that keeps women in the home — is an unchanging, divinely ordained institution. Rather, feminist scholars assert that gender and sexual relations are socially constructed over time — not the inevitable outcome of biology or "God's plan for the world." Through European colonization and Catholic missionary activity, Catholic ideology has been transplanted to many parts of the world. Anthropologist Eleanor Leacock and sociologist Karen Anderson are two scholars who have researched the imposition of Catholicism's celebrated "divine plan" for marriage and the family in Canada. Correspondence from the seventeenth and eighteenth centuries between Jesuit missionaries and their superiors in France suggests that the Jesuits imposed Catholic marriage and family relations upon the Huron and Montagnais as they had developed among Catholics in France. According to Leacock the introduction of a European family structure, with male authority, female fidelity and the elimination of the right to divorce, was essential to the Jesuit program.[19] Similarly, Anderson tells us,

> In seeking to transform both Huron and Montagnais societies, the Jesuits acted from a body of knowledge (Christian Theology) which viewed the proper ordering of relations between people as decidedly hierarchical, and which attributed specific and different natures and capabilities to men and women ... In carrying out their missions to the Hurons and Montagnais, the Jesuits sought to put that body of knowledge into practice by convincing the native peoples of New France that Christianity embodied the true expression of the nature of men and women.[20]

Although Catholics are no longer burning women at the stake or taking such overt measures to convert and proselytize as in centuries past, the basic structure of male dominance within the contemporary Catholic church remains largely unchallenged.[21] One example is Pope John Paul II's recent reference to "radical feminism" as an obstacle to "the family." A 1995 news item reported: "Pope John Paul II said Sunday society should place greater value on the role women play in the home and suggested the influence of radical feminism is on the wane."[22] In contemporary western societies, the emergence of the pro-family movement has played an important role in the effort to retain patriarchal family values. The pro-family movement identifies feminism and the secularization of culture as among the most serious threats to the realization of "God's plan" for "the family." Included within this umbrella movement are Realwomen of Canada, a women's group that seeks to protect women's traditional roles as wives and mothers,[23] and the Promise Keepers, a Christian men's group that encourages men to reclaim their role as leaders of church, home and society.[24] Among Catholics, the pro-family movement includes the anti-abortion campaign called "Right to Life." Rosemary Radford Ruether argues that

> the very name by which this group refers to itself — "Right to Life" — is misleading, since these groups have very little concern for "life" in the broader sense. They happily support capital punishment and war, and they show little interest in the economic survival of children after birth ... It is not primitive ignorance but patriarchal ideology that decrees that women should not use contraceptives or seek abortion and should accept whatever pregnancies "God" and males impose on them.[25]

Even with Vatican II, and the call for openness that char-acterized its implementation, Catholic sexual and family ide-ology remains fundamentally the same. Why do today's proponents of the pro-family movement and today's official Catholic church feel threatened by demands for changes to Catholicism's "theology" of sexuality and gender relations in families? In other words, why does the church refuse to alter its rigid sexual ideology and insist on supporting, as natural and divinely ordained, a division of labour that keeps women in the home? It seems to be in part because members of the Catholic ruling apparatus have a vested interest in maintaining patriarchal privilege; by keeping "the family" strong, limiting women's opportunities to achieve economic independence and denying women the autonomy to deter-mine our own reproductive futures Catholicism retains its control over women.

Throughout history, patriarchy has been integral to Catholicism and the Christian tradition as a whole. Yet while the Catholic church's official position may not be changing, Catholic family culture (and the way that Catholicism is practiced) is in transition. The second half of the twentieth century has witnessed profound changes in the efficacy of re-ligious ideology, including Catholic ideology, within Cana-dian society and beyond. Feminist scholars remind us that patriarchy is *not* inevitable. Feminists have examined many social forces — the media, our capitalist economy and our legal system, to name just a few — that shape gender and sexual relations, but the impact of religious ideology has been under-explored. By advancing our understanding of the links between Christianity and abuses of many kinds, femi-nist scholars are giving us the tools to resist and transform religious ideology. In the next chapter I explore how this transition in Catholic family culture helped to create an awareness of fault lines in Catholic women's lives as they found the right time in history to break the silence about incest.

Chapter 5

Charting Fault Lines
in Catholic Family Culture

At the fault line along which women's experience breaks away from the discourses mediated by texts that are integral to the relations of ruling in contemporary society, a critical standpoint emerges. *We make a new language that gives us speech, ways of knowing, ways of working politically.*[1]
— Dorothy E. Smith

∾

You have this idea of what you were like as a child and how you grew up and that's your view of reality. But when you start to remember the abuse that view just cracks. I don't know how else to describe it. It's like a fissure goes right through reality — and what looked like reality you realize wasn't reality at all.   — Faye

Repressing the memories? It's like you had a tape recorder — you rewind it, it's gone.   — Mary

THESE DAYS "INCEST" and "sexual abuse" are commonplace terms. But today's awareness was clearly lacking in earlier decades, especially prior to the 1980s. (As Mary said in an interview, "Everyone knows that sexual abuse is illegal — it'd be hard to live in a cocoon today.") What has happened in the last ten to fifteen years to bring incest and sexual abuse into our everyday consciousness? Why is it suddenly the right time in history for us to grapple with how and why sexual abuse occurs? What are some of overall shifts that have helped us — as a society — to open our eyes to child sexual abuse?

The process by which the eight participants identified themselves, at the right time in their own life histories, as survivors of incest helps us chart these shifts. As part of a "generation" of people who have "come out" as survivors of sexual abuse, each of these eight women, in identifying herself as an incest survivor, allowed for the emergence of a life-changing *critical standpoint* on the world. (Recall Elizabeth's words: "Uncovering that history of abuse was really life-changing — I couldn't look at *anything* the same way again.") Their critical standpoints were influenced in significant ways by their experiences of Catholic family culture. Their incest histories, then, can be thought of as ruptures or fault lines within this culture. An exploration of their resistance helps us to see how these women have countered not only society's overall patriarchal ideology but, more specifically, Catholic family and sexual ideology.

The stories of these eight women support the view that, prior to second-wave feminism and Catholicism's second Vatican Council (commonly known as Vatican II), Catholic family culture (and Canadian society as a whole) supported neither an awareness of family violence nor the measures to ensure protection against it. But in many parts of the western world, and certainly in Canada, Catholic culture has changed considerably since the 1960s.[2] Changes implemented as a result of Vatican II inadvertently opened Catholic family culture to secular influences. Among these influences were second-wave feminism, women's changing socio-economic status within society and an increase in our society's consciousness about family violence. Together, these influences helped to weaken the salience and impact of Catholic family and sexual ideology.

During the 1940s and 1950s we, as a society, repressed our knowledge of family violence (especially its more insidious forms such as incest) despite the fact that violence was widespread in families. As a social phenomenon that affected the individual survivors as well as society as a whole, our collective repression of violence against women and children captures the essence of Dorothy Smith's claim that ideological practices, and their concomitant forms of consciousness, alienate women from their own experience. So why *did* we repress this knowledge? In short, because it wasn't the right time in history to deal with it — the historical and material conditions did not support an overall awareness of family violence.

In *The Conceptual Practices of Power,* Dorothy Smith emphasizes that fault lines in women's lives become visible only when the historical and material conditions support their emergence. Gillian Walker, in her analysis of Canadian women's resistance to family violence, similarly stresses that the right historical and material conditions allow for the voicing of counter-hegemonic ideas:

> Although in various ways those who rule strive to maintain what Gramsci has characterized as ideological hegemony, the process by which social reality is constructed results in there being considerable discrepancy and disjunction between the ideological forms provided for us to understand the world and our direct experience of our situation in that world. These gaps and disjunctions have,

under particular historic considerations and in certain sites, allowed for the voicing of "counter-hegemonic" ideas and the taking of action by those who feel that they are not being governed by their own best interests.[3]

The historical and material conditions of the 1940s and 1950s certainly did not allow for the voicing of "counter-hegemonic ideas" — ideas that would help women to challenge oppressive family structures and practices. Canada's legal system unquestionably gave men the upper hand (as late as 1970, Quebec was the only Canadian province granting women equal status with men in questions of matrimonial property rights[4]). Women had limited access to high-paying employment. Within universities and the government bodies that regulated social policy, the voices of women were rarely heard or considered. Popular culture, epitomized by TV sitcoms such as "Father Knows Best" (which won an award in 1955 for its "constructive portrayal of American family life"[5]), encouraged patriarchal privilege and selfless feminine domesticity in countless ways. And during these decades, there were no shelters and safe houses for women and children seeking refuge from violence. Women who were caught in violent family situations had no recourse but to make the best of very difficult situations.

During these decades, religious ideological practices were clearly also among the complex cluster of practices enforcing the "institution of compulsory heterosexuality"[6] within Canadian society. In significant ways during these decades Catholic ideology *compounded* these prevalent secular practices by adding a moral dimension to them. In other words, having "God" endorse a conservative family structure made such a family structure seem divinely ordained and, therefore, unchallengeable.[7]

Second-Wave Feminism

The 1960s marked the beginnings of great change in western culture. Second-wave feminism was a primary catalyst in this far-reaching social change; its consciousness-raising played a key role in bringing family violence into our everyday consciousness. The era of second-wave feminism was characterized by an dynamic interplay between, on the one hand, changes in women's socio-economic status in Canadian society, and, on the other hand, women's increasing consciousness about discrimination and violence in their myriad forms. As women became conscious of the ways in which their everyday/everynight experiences broke away from patriarchal practices and forms of consciousness, they named the acts of violence that had hitherto been repressed and denied. Women began (to use Dorothy Smith's metaphor) to identify the fault lines in their lives. Doing so permitted the emergence of critical standpoints on society and gave voice to counter-hegemonic ideas and practices. Faye, for instance, said that remembering her history of incest was like a "fissure" — an image that mirrors Dorothy Smith's metaphor of a line of fault — cutting through what she had *thought* was reality:

> You have this idea of what you were like as a child and how you grew up and that's your view of reality. But when you start to remember abuse that view just cracks. I don't know how else to describe it. It's like a fissure goes right through reality and what looked like reality you realize wasn't reality at all. And it makes you feel crazy until you start to sort that out and work through things and you're able to talk about it. It feels like you're crazy, like you're losing your mind. So I think what happened was that women would have that experience, feeling like they were

going crazy and they'd be treated as crazy — until they started realizing they were starting to get in touch with reality, and that the illusion was what was cracking, not reality.

VATICAN II

Contemporaneous with (though independent of) the emergence of second-wave feminism in the 1960s, Catholicism's second Vatican Council set out to revise Catholic church practices.[8] In one of her interviews, Mary said the changes brought on by Vatican II "opened a window where before all the windows had been closed." Dramatic changes were implemented. Lay people came to be viewed as at least as important as the clergy and institutional hierarchy — a change that directly challenged previous understandings of "church." The liturgy was reformed. (Priests, for example, no longer said mass in Latin but in the vernacular.) Lay people, including women, began to take a more active role in mass and the overall activity of the church. And Vatican II encouraged Catholics to be less concerned to follow Catholicism's "rules" and more concerned to follow the "spirit" of Catholicism. Faye told me:

> After Vatican II the emphasis was supposed to be on the spirit of the church and on developing a relationship with God. In pre–Vatican II times that was unheard of. That would have been considered presumptuous. The priests were supposed to mediate between the people and God. That was one of the major shifts — the idea that people themselves would have a relationship with God. Ordinary people, not saints. Just ordinary people were expected to have a relationship with God and it wasn't mediated through the priests.

Despite Vatican II's aim to bring the Catholic church up to date with contemporary culture, Vatican II did not lead to substantive changes in official Catholic teachings on marriage, sexuality and the family — what I have identified in previous chapters as Catholic family and sexual ideology. However, the rhetoric did shift slightly.[9] Although Catholic documents written before the 1960s upheld an unapologetically patriarchal model of family life, in which father is head, mother is subordinate and children are obedient to both, Catholic documents written in recent decades uphold patriarchal ideology in subtler ways. The pre– and post–Vatican II positions correspond to the two basic forms of conservativism:

> Conservatives either claim that the female role is not inferior to that of men [the post–Vatican II position], or they argue that women are inherently better adapted than men to the traditional female sex role [the pre–Vatican II position]. The former claim advocates a kind of sexual apartheid, typically described by such phrases as "complementary but equal"; the latter postulates an inherent inequality between the sexes.[10]

Catholic documents written prior to Vatican II represent the classical conservative view of the family, that women are inherently inferior to men, while post–Vatican II documents endorse a cornerstone of classical liberalism: equality. Pope John Paul II's 1981 exhortation on marriage and the family, for example, argues for the *formal* equality of spouses. But the exhortation, which includes a section devoted to women's place in society, states that "the true advancement of women requires that clear recognition be given to the value of their maternal and family role, by comparison with all other public roles."[11] Fundamentally, then, there is a hollowness in the claim of women's equality with men: the official Catholic church still clearly promotes as "God's plan" a family structure that supports the institution of compulsory heterosexuality: permanent and indissoluble marriage, a procreative, anti-contraceptive sexual ethic, and a division of labour in which men earn the family wage while women perform the unpaid labour related to the care of children and home.

In spite of the lack of change in *official* church teaching on marriage and the family since the 1960s, the way Catholics actually *practice* their faith — the widespread use of birth control among Catholics, for example — has undergone an enormous transition. Mary Jo Leddy, a prominent Canadian Catholic, suggested in a recent book: "I think that for ten years, despite the official teaching of the Church, at least 85 or 90 per cent of the Catholic population has been practicing birth control. It's clear that their value system is exactly the same as that of people who are not part of the Church."[12]

When I talked to the participants about Vatican II, they agreed among themselves that the efficacy of Catholic family culture seemed to be weakened by second-wave feminism. Faye, for example, attributed changes in the attitudes of post–Vatican II Catholics — and the increased awareness of sexual abuse — to the women's movement:

> I think attitudes towards sexuality have changed in post–Vatican II times and that helped to bring sexual abuse out of the closet. Our culture had changed to the point where it started to become common knowledge. And I think the whole culture went through a re-emergence of memories in the sense of breaking down barriers of repression. It wasn't just an individual thing. I think it was happening to us as individuals but it was because of the whole culture. I think the women's movement was the biggest influence. I don't think any of this stuff would have come out

if it hadn't been for the women's movement. It was finally giving a voice to women — women speaking up.

CATHOLIC IDEOLOGY AND HISTORICAL MATERIALISM

For both the pre– and post–Vatican II participants — Elizabeth, Cherrie, Faye and Mary who grew up prior to Vatican II and Courage, Maya, Content and Jackie who grew up after Vatican II — Catholic ideological practices clearly shaped everyday/everynight family relations. While the effects of Catholic ideology were more extreme for the pre–Vatican II participants, in all eight families Catholic ideology depended upon Catholic identity as a means of social control. In other words, "good" Catholics were rewarded for their conformity to the gender and sexual roles idealized by Catholic ideology. The strength of Catholic ideology depended on these Catholic identities. Catholic wives and mothers, for instance, were expected to emulate the Virgin Mary — especially the Virgin Mary's selflessness, compliance and sexual purity. (Recall that the Virgin Mary's contradictory status as both virgin and mother is an impossible ideal for "actual" women to achieve.)

Catholic ideology functioned as an honour and shame code. An honour and shame code refers to a system of social control in which a community evaluates its members by a set of relatively unambiguous standards.[13] In these eight families, the "set of relatively unambiguous standards" was Catholic family and sexual ideology. In an interview, Mary recalled an incident that illustrates the point:

> One thing led to another with [my then boyfriend] and one night we wound up having intercourse. Wouldn't you know, I was pregnant! Very fertile people this whole family,

good at producing children! Anyway, I knew that Frank
didn't want to get married. Being a good Catholic I went
to a priest and told him about it. He said, "You'll have to
honour that. You'll have to get married." That priest is
dead now or would I ever give him a tongue-lashing! He
said, "Make sure you're pregnant and then I'll look him
up." The priest went up to the school where Frank was
teaching and told the principal he had to see him. He said
to Frank, *"What are you going to do to redeem this woman's
honour?"* The priest just said he owed this to me, that he'd
have to marry me. Of course, Frank said, "Ya, I'll marry
her." What can you say? Here's a priest with shotgun to
your head! Ohh! Isn't that terrible?

When I asked the women how Catholic family culture
shaped their specific experiences of incest, all eight participants told me that the dominant forms of Catholic consciousness supported neither a critical awareness of incest as a form
of abuse, nor, as a consequence, the language and measures to
put a stop to it. In fact, all four of the pre–Vatican II women,
Elizabeth, Cherrie, Faye and Mary, completely repressed their
memories of incest until well into their forties (that is, until
various times between the mid-1980s to early 1990s). Faye
told us that, in the pre–Vatican II era, incest would have been
considered just as "horrifying and unthinkable" as the notion
that sexual abuse could be perpetrated by a priest. As a result,
she simply blocked out what was happening with her father:

> The idea that incest would ever happen in Catholic fami-
> lies was horrifying and unthinkable. It would never even
> cross people's minds that such a thing could happen. And
> even suggesting that it could would just be tantamount to
> heresy. It was so unthinkable that something like that
> could ever happen that I just didn't think about it. It's not

like I even remember wondering if other kids had the same thing happen. I just didn't think about it. I completely blocked it out.

Courage, Maya, Content and Jackie, on the other hand, did not as thoroughly block out their memories of abuse. Yet for all eight women, the memories were "tucked away" and "ignored" until they felt safe enough to explore them.

Dorothy Smith's historical materialist framework helps to explain their silences. Smith adopts a critical insight of Marx and Engels to show how

> the ideas produced by a ruling class may dominate and penetrate the social consciousness of the society in general, and thus may effectively control the social process of consciousness in ways that deny expression to the actual experience people have ... of their everyday world ... Ideology builds the internal social organization of the ruling class as well as its domination over others. Its overall character, however, *depends upon, and takes for granted, the social relations that organize and enforce the silences of those who do not participate in the process, who are outside it* [emphasis added].[14]

As I reflected with the women on their life stories, I was reminded that the success and efficacy of Catholic ideology has *depended upon and taken for granted* the silence of those outside the ruling apparatus. Breaking the silence about incest exposed the fault lines between the women's experiences of incest and the dominant forms of consciousness in these Catholic families. Breaking the silence acted against a family culture that alienated women from their own experience.[15]

But for the pre–Vatican II participants who grew up during the 1940s and 1950s, the process of breaking silence simply could not have occurred. At a time when incest formed no part of the society's everyday consciousness, these four incest survivors not only had no recourse in putting a stop to it, they lacked the language to describe their experiences. Repressing their memories was the only alternative. They were therefore *profoundly* alienated from their actual everyday/everynight experiences of incest. What compounded the repression of their memories was undoubtedly the fact that all four pre–Vatican II women were sexually abused by their fathers (and, in at least three of these cases, by other family members as well). Incest between a father and daughter has been found to be the most traumatic and strongly linked to the repression of memories.[16] For Mary, repressing the knowledge of her father's violations was a way to "live with [the abuser] day to day and not go insane":

> My counsellor and I figured that I'd so thoroughly repressed all this [until my 40s] because he was my father. I couldn't afford to have the memory. So I forgot every single incident and each occasion would be brand new. And, of course, during recollection I had asthma again [as in childhood]. I think that's the difference between it being ordinary sexual abuse and it being a parent or a close relative like a brother. Because you can't live with them and keep that memory. Putting the memory aside you can still live with them day to day and not go insane. I think that's how we very cleverly kept our sanity.

For the younger generation of women, the lines of fault — their incest histories — became visible earlier in their lives. Their early self-identification as incest survivors was supported by the interplay between women's increased consciousness about family violence after the 1960s and the changing material and socio-economic conditions for women that supported this emergent consciousness. For example, Maya's decision to really look at her 1970s incest history was influenced by changes in society as a whole (sexual abuse talked about in the media) as well as changes in her economic status:

> My memories were never really totally blocked out but I can remember clearly when I really started to think about them again. It wasn't that I forgot them, it's just that I kind of ignored them for a long time. I think I became more aware of the abuse in my late teens when it started to be more around in the media. On a personal level there were also some circumstances like being able to have a job that enabled me to leave the house which in turn enabled me to have a more objective, clear-sighted view of what had gone on in the family. If I hadn't gotten a job I probably would've stayed at home and wouldn't have been able to go to therapy as consistently. And it really helped not having to play a game, not having to play nicey-nicey, buying into this façade that nothing had happened to me.

For Jackie, the link between second-wave feminism and her "coming out" as a survivor was clear. Her first moment of identification occurred while she attended a workshop sponsored by the feminist group at her university: "I had never thought of myself as a survivor before I started getting involved in the women's group on campus. I guess I knew I had been sexually abused but I never considered myself a survivor."

And for Faye, who began to recall her memories of incest around 1990, an important condition for feeling safe enough to remember was her father's death:

> I think one very, very important part of that was my father dying. I don't think it was safe for me to remember before

that. I spent a lot of time with my father before he died and it was positive in the sense that seeing him really sick, I lost the sense of being afraid of him. But I didn't really start to remember until after he died. Then it was safe to remember.

At various historical moments in the past decade, then, these eight women came to identify themselves as incest survivors. Doing so broke the silence about their abuse and marked the emergence of a resistance to social forms of consciousness that had worked to alienate them from their experiences of incest. Giving a voice to the incest, and doing the emotional work that followed, transformed their alienation. As Dorothy Smith suggests, giving voice to the fault lines in our lives provides

> an opening in a discursive fabric through which a range of [experience] hitherto denied, repressed, subordinated, and absent to and lacking language, can break out ... The opening up of women's experience gives [us] access to social realities previously unavailable, indeed repressed.[17]

From the collective standpoint of these incest survivors a central contradiction emerged. Why, when Catholic ideology promised (and continues to promise) the full realization of dignity for every family member within a traditional Catholic family structure, was there so much disempowerment and so much shame and denial about sexuality in these eight families? Together, the eight participants and I charted three significant points of rupture within Catholic family culture — points at which their *actually lived* everyday/everynight childhood experiences broke away from Catholic family and sexual ideology:

1. Catholic family ideology assumed that males in families could enact and adopt positions of social privilege without threatening the dignity and empowerment of other family members (notably wives and children). In these Catholic families such an assumption was unfounded. The women strongly linked their incest histories to male social privilege.

2. Catholic family ideology assumed that families in which women were limited to their roles as wives and mothers would foster the full dignity of every family member. Such was not the case in these Catholic families. On the contrary, the mothers' vulnerable socio-economic status seemed to work in concert with their identities as "good Catholic wives and mothers" to prevent mothers from supporting their daughters. In other words, mothers were forced to choose between, on the one hand, the dictates for "good" Catholic wives and mothers — placing husband and marriage before all else — and, on the other hand, their daughters' and their own dignity and safety.

3. Catholic sexual ideology's rigid regulation of sexuality, along with the profound repercussions for "immoral" sexual behaviour, worked against the survivors by creating a culture of *erotophobia* — a culture in which fear, denial of and punishment for sexuality were the norm. Further, the very act of incest, which constituted a serious breach of Catholic sexual ideology, compounded the survivors' feelings of unworthiness, guilt and self-blame.

In the next three chapters I draw on the women's experiences to explore these points of rupture. From their collective standpoint we begin to develop a "new language that gives us speech, ways of knowing, ways of working politically"[18] to make families more empowering for women and children.

Chapter 6

CATHOLIC FAMILY IDEOLOGY, MALE PRIVILEGE AND INCEST

All of man's natural aggressiveness, his masculine brawn, his logical mind, make being head easy for him. What is more, nothing gives a man greater satisfaction than a realized sense of importance. Men want recognition. They thrive on it. And their natural instinct in marriage is to be head. If they abdicate the masculine role in the family, they feel guilty; if they are denied it, they are resentful. Nothing like this is natural to the woman.[1]

— The Reverend George A. Kelly,
The Catholic Marriage Manual, 1958

∾

On Sunday we'd go to church but Saturday night Dad would drink, smash the old lady up, smash us around and the next day we'd be in church with the Sunday little white gloves on. I still remember those little white gloves. It's so ironic. It was like "The Gong Show" but to everyone else we were a happy, normal family.   — Courage

When [my stepfather] told me to do something I had to do it. He was the adult and I was the child.   — Jackie

I didn't have any boundaries ... I had no rights — it wasn't okay to state your needs. There was no sanctity of the person.   — Elizabeth

The whole idea was that the father of the family, the man of the family or the husband, represented God in the family. I can remember we used to have sermons on those kind of topics regularly, how the man in the family represented God so that you were supposed to have the same attitude towards them that you would have towards God. There was no need to talk about it — it was just the way things were.   — Faye

I had a lot of anger at God for not saving me from this.
                            — Mary

THE STANDPOINT OF THESE eight women powerfully suggests that Catholic family practices (especially prior to Vatican II in the 1960s) endorsed male privilege. In our discussions, we found that, in their experience, male privilege more often supported the violation of women and children in families than their protection, as official Catholic teachings claimed. Far from being unpredictable and random acts of violence, the incest these women endured was clearly influenced by a complex interplay of family ideological practices, including children's enforced, unquestioning obedience, men's lack of respect for personal boundaries, a fear of male authority that impeded attempts to put a stop to the incest and "Father God" imagery that compounded the survivors' already profound feelings of alienation and betrayal. We can learn a lot about these incest histories by contrasting official Catholic teachings on the family — paying particular attention to their prescribed roles for men — with some everyday/everynight experiences of male privilege in Catholic families.

MALE PRIVILEGE: OFFICIAL CATHOLIC TEACHINGS

Catholic teachings have always promoted the twofold belief that male privilege is imprinted in the "nature" of human beings, and that God created a world in which women and children were meant to be dominated by men. Historically, this twofold belief manifested itself not only within Catholicism's institutional hierarchy but also within Catholic families. As earthly patriarchs, both priests and fathers were thought to be the representatives of God the Father, the divine patriarch. The belief that male dominance is natural and part of "God's plan" for the world provided a theological foundation for Catholic teachings on marriage and the family, teachings that have carried into the present day.

Pope Leo XIII, in his 1880 encyclical On Christian Marriage, stated explicitly:

> The man is the chief of the family, and the head of the woman, who nevertheless, inasmuch as she is flesh of his flesh, and bone of his bone, should be subject to and obey the man, not as a servant, but as a companion; and so neither honour nor dignity is lost by the rendering of obedience.[2]

In a similar vein, the 1958 Catholic Marriage Manual assured its readers not only that a man has a natural inclination to be head of the family but that a woman "wants to be dominated by her husband."[3] The influential manual made official church teachings accessible through its use of everyday language. Its aim was to help Catholic couples navigate the often troubled waters of married life — but in a way that celebrated male dominance and women's natural inclination for marriage and motherhood. And having received the official church stamps *nihil obstat* and *imprimatur* ("nothing standing in the way" and "let it be printed"[4]), the book assured Catholics that its contents were free of doctrinal error. The Reverend George A. Kelly expounded:

> All of man's natural aggressiveness, his masculine brawn, his logical mind, make being head easy for him. What is more, nothing gives a man greater satisfaction than a realized sense of importance. Men want recognition. They thrive on it. And their natural instinct in marriage is to be head. If they abdicate the masculine role in the family, they feel guilty; if they are denied it, they are resentful. Nothing like this is natural to the woman.[5]

The marriage manual emphasized that domestic quarrels should be settled according to the "proper" roles assigned "by God" to husbands and wives:

> When you as a husband recognize that your wife needs to express herself emotionally and intuitively, you take a long step toward accepting her for what she is — a woman. When you recognize your husband's need to express himself forcefully and sometimes boisterously, you accept him for what he is — a man. Many troubles encountered by modern couples result from a husband's unwillingness to encourage his wife to be a woman, and from the wife's unwillingness to let her man fulfill the masculine role assigned to him by God ... A wife must allow her husband to assume his full prerogatives as the male; a husband must

encourage his wife to be feminine. In no other way can two persons achieve their maximum potential in marriage.[6]

And the role assigned to children in the ideal Catholic family has been one of obedience and respect toward their parents. Pope Leo XIII stated:

> As regards to children, they are bound to obey and be subject to their parents, and to do them honour for conscience sake; and, on the other hand, every care and forethought should be vigilantly exercised by parents to protect their children and train them to virtue: "Fathers bring [your children] ... up in the discipline and the correction of the Lord."[7]

John Paul II's demand for children's obedience is not significantly different from Leo XIII's message given more than one hundred years earlier:

> All members of the family, each according to his or her own gift, have the grace and responsibility of building day by day the communion of persons, making the family "a school of deeper humanity" ... By means of love, respect and obedience to their parents, children offer their specific and irreplaceable contribution to the construction of an authentically human and Christian family.[8]

At the same time, Catholic teachings assume that the positive side of patriarchal values — love, loyalty and the protection of family members under their care — naturally flows from the roles assigned to men as husbands and fathers. In 1981 John Paul II explained that "love for his wife as mother of their children and love for the children themselves are for the man the natural way of understanding and fulfilling his own fatherhood."[9]

Official church teachings, then, have consistently promoted a hierarchy of social privilege within the ideal Catholic family: children defer to parents, women defer to men and men assume a natural and rightful position as the head of the family. At the same time, the official church has been conscious of the fact that *actual* family structures, in various times and cultures, have differed from this patriarchal ideal. So Catholics have been told to counter forces in society — feminism being a prime example — that create obstacles to the development of the family structure God "intends" for human beings. Catholics are warned "to set themselves in opposition" to the sinful corruption of "fundamental values" in contemporary society — especially an increase in the rate of divorce, the widespread use of artificial contraceptives and the prevalence of extramarital sex — which, according to the official church, are threatening "the family's full realization of itself."[10]

But feminists have long been asking: From whose standpoint is this an *ideal* family structure? Whose interests are served within it?

THE INCEST HISTORIES:
CATHOLIC FAMILY IDEOLOGY AND MALE PRIVILEGE

From the standpoint of every woman I interviewed, the dominant family ideology demanded adherence to a hierarchy of social privilege in which men unquestionably assumed a "one-up" position. Although Catholicism was only one factor among many that influenced the dominant family ideology, it clearly reinforced hierarchical family relations and the forms of consciousness that supported them. Maya's family was typical. Her parents, who were brought up during the decades of strict 1940s and 1950s Catholicism, sought to emulate Catholic family teachings and to pass on Catholic values to their children. From her standpoint in the family, an unquestioning acceptance of traditional gender roles meant that her father regularly made unilateral decisions and failed to respect his wife's dreams and goals:

> My parents had different backgrounds but one of the strongest things they had in common was that they were both Catholic. I think the [Catholic] tradition was so ingrained that they wouldn't have even realized they were making decisions based on this. The expected [gender] roles were so taken for granted, like second nature. Dad didn't respect Mom. I have a lot of anger about the way he treated her. He didn't respect her dreams and her goals and her way of life. She ended up going to work after having six children, partly because of economic necessity and partly because she felt so unfulfilled living in the country, struggling to be a housewife with this guy who had impossible standards of housekeeping. My dad definitely saw domestic labour as the mother's role.

Overall, the experiences of these eight women reveal official Catholic *teachings* to be a form of ruling *ideology* — an interplay of beliefs and practices that enable men to sustain their dominance over women and children. Everyday/ everynight family practices fostered an acceptance of male privilege that was difficult, and often impossible, to challenge.

The structure of each family conformed to the Catholic family "ideal." The families were undeniably Catholic; they were also undeniably patriarchal. Courage's struggle, for example, to overcome her 1960s and 1970s childhood of abuse led her to the conclusion that the many forms of violence in her family — physical and emotional as well as sexual —

were linked to the lack of respect for anyone else who occupied a "one-down" position on the family hierarchy. Courage emphasized the disjuncture between her family's outward appearance — that they were "good Catholics" because they attended mass each week — and the violence that was part of their everyday/everynight family life:

> I mean, on Sunday we'd go to church but Saturday night Dad would drink, smash the old lady up, smash us around and the next day we'd be in church with the Sunday little white gloves on. I still remember those little white gloves. It's so ironic. It was like "The Gong Show" but to everyone else we were a happy, normal family.

In all eight families, fathers (with the exception of Jackie's family in which her stepfather took on the fathering role) acted as the primary or sole breadwinners while mothers assumed primary responsibility for unpaid childcare and domestic labour. This family structure, and the beliefs and practices that supported it, were linked with the incest histories in important ways.

MALE PRIVILEGE: PROTECTION OR VIOLATION?

Official Catholic teachings claim that a man's position as "head of the family" is the natural way for men to protect the family members under their care. But these eight women agreed that male privilege more often led to violation of women and children than their protection. During the years that Maya was sexually abused by her father's brother, the fear of her father overshadowed her desire to seek protection from him. In this way, her father's position worked against her attempts to stop the incest. There was an obvious disjuncture between what was *supposed* to be happening in this "good" Catholic family and, in Maya's words, "the real picture of what was going on":

> Both Cecil [my uncle] and I were really afraid of my dad — Cecil because Dad was his older brother, me because he was my father. He was the disciplinarian and occasionally used physical violence for punishment. We were all just really afraid to cross him. He was a harder disciplinarian than Mom — concrete threats were pervasive. In terms of my dad finding out [about the incest], a lot of it was just plain fear of physical punishment and emotional punishment from my dad. There's a part of me that always wanted to be able to go to Dad so that he'd protect me but my stronger feeling was fear. The ideal was the father as this benevolent ruler of the family and his power was supposed to be a good thing but in my family Dad's power was based on fear rather than respect — and he abused his power. My father's power as the figurehead of the family was enabled by people's *fear* of him rather than people's *respect* for him. So the real picture of what was going on was that this hierarchy was there, like in the ideal Catholic family, but it was not a good thing — it was based on fear and the power was abused. It enabled the abuse because, you know, here's this person who's supposed to protect me and I can't tell him what's going on with my uncle because I'm scared to death he's going to punish me. That's really how the power was working whereas the ideal picture is like, he's your dad and he'll take care of you, he takes care of the whole family.

The privilege granted to fathers, older brothers, uncles and stepfathers fostered many forms of violations — from inappropriate touching and sexual remarks to wife battering and sex between fathers and their daughters. The dominant forms of consciousness meant, quite simply, that the desires and needs of males were "respected" while females were expected to sacrifice their own. Around 1950, Elizabeth experienced a devastating violation at the hands of her father:

> The incest with my dad first happened when we were taking a trip. We stopped overnight although we didn't really have to, I mean, it wasn't really necessary. I guess I was thirteen or fourteen. He took me to supper and then to a movie. You know, I can still remember the movie and the actress. Then we went back to the hotel. I remember the room, too, it was small and crowded, and it had a sink but it didn't have a toilet. The window beside the bed faced the street. And I still remember the pyjamas I was wearing. There was a double bed although I don't think I even questioned it at the time, I don't remember feeling odd about it at all. The fact that I didn't means he probably had never done anything like this to me before. He locked the door behind him and told me he was going downstairs for a while. I knew he was going down to the bar. He locked the door so I'd be safe. I was really scared all alone in the hotel room because I wasn't used to being alone in strange places. I don't know what time he came up but I knew he'd been drinking. I didn't want to talk with him, it always used to bother me a lot when he was drinking. He undressed and probably kept his underwear on and then he came right up to me. I remember him fondling my breasts and ejaculating on my lower back — no wonder I have lower back pain today! I pretended I was asleep and stayed there till I fell asleep. I didn't dare move. The next morning it was as if nothing had happened.

The encounter highlights a bitter irony: that at the same time as her father took measures to ensure her protection, presumably from other men ("he locked the door so I'd be safe"), he himself took on the role of violator.

Faye's account of an ongoing incestuous relationship with her father is an example of a sexual violation that had lasting and painfully confusing repercussions. For Faye, her father's roles as protector and violator were inextricably bound together. On one hand he was cruel and fearsome, on the other hand, he was a vital source of security and affection:

> I was physically afraid of my father, I mean I was afraid of the "Bad One." He was very physically cruel in some ways. I had to perform oral sex on him and he performed some kind of anal sex on me too. That was really horrible. It gives me chills thinking about it again. So I was afraid of him hurting me again because he had hurt me, lots of times before. But at the same time for me not to have that special relationship with my father would have been total and utter abandonment. He was my main source of affection because, I mean, my mother was completely detached from me. So the idea of not having that special relationship was unbearable. There would have been too much to lose. On one hand I was afraid of him but on the other hand I adored him. My relationship with my father had repercussions in every sexual relationship with a man — the shame, the degradation, somehow the knowledge that I was utterly irredeemable because of this. But there was another side to it too, a kind of romantic, special feeling. Because this was a secret relationship that only we shared. That part was really seductive. And later when I was trying to work all this stuff out, the good and the bad were intertwined, the feelings of violation, the feelings of

specialness, all at the same time and it made things painfully complicated for me.

Maya, who was sexually abused by her father's brother over several years, also described her father's failure to respect her personal boundaries. Her father's "confused attempts at being affectionate" pushed the boundary of protection and support into the realm of personal violation:

Not only Dad's physical punishments felt like a boundary crossing but also his signs of affection would often take me by surprise. Like he'd come up behind me and put his hand on my neck and to this day I can't stand anyone putting their hand on my neck. [It felt] really possessive and abrupt and it was something that didn't feel good, like it wasn't gentle. He also made confused attempts at being affectionate but they had sexual overtones and they made me really uncomfortable — talking about my appearance all the time. Whether the comments were positive or negative they were intrusive and unwelcome, sort of none of his business — but he *made* it his business.

The change in the role of Content's father from protector to violator was also evident. She told me how her father tried to control her and her sisters' intimate relationships:

The boys were allowed to come and go to town as they pleased. But for my sisters and I it was a different story. Guys would call the house but we weren't allowed to talk to them on the phone. And if we went to town to meet a guy we had to say we were going to a friend's house overnight. We'd have to lie all the time. Every time a guy called me on the phone, he was always listening on the other end. It was embarrassing, especially when the guy'd be on the other end and I'd be saying, "Dad, get off the phone!" Or I'd say, "Just a minute," and I'd put down the phone and catch him on the other end hanging it up. But then I know darn well he'd pick it up again. So it was really embarrassing. I wasn't allowed to go to town at the time and go to the movies so I don't know whether he thought the guy was going to ask me to have sex on the phone or something, I don't know.

OBEDIENCE

Obedience was another important part of the dominant family ideology. While Catholic family ideology claims that children's obedience provides the groundwork for "authentically human and Christian" family life,[11] the standpoint of these women suggests that unquestioning obedience to male authority fostered incest. Faye was sexually abused by her father during the decades preceding Vatican II. Obedience and loyalty to her father were among the strongest reasons that she never told anyone about the abuse:

> It started at such a young age that by the time I realized it was wrong it had been going on for so long that I felt I couldn't tell anyone about it. I felt responsible for it, the badness of it, I mean. Something bad was going on and my assumption was that it was my badness. After all, fathers were supposed to be like God so it couldn't be my father who was the bad one. My loyalty was to my father — this was our secret and he said nobody else would understand. So, ya, mostly it was loyalty and obedience to my father. It's hard to get back into the mind of a little child. I mean, I'm sure I never actually had those specific thoughts. But in hindsight that feeling of loyalty was very

strong. It was just part of the overall cultural ethos that pervaded the atmosphere. Men were powerful and that's just the way things were.

As in Faye's case, Mary's experiences of pre–Vatican II Catholicism (in her home, in school and at church) demanded that she obey her parents and other authority figures, especially priests and nuns. This helped to silence her. "You know, you respect your parents so thoroughly you wouldn't dare tell on them. Parents represented authority and the church and everything good." For Mary, the dominant belief about parents — that they represent "everything good" — left no room for identifying parental abuse. The fact that Mary's father had sex with her many times over a number of years obviously contradicted that belief.

Jackie, who was sexually abused during the 1970s and into the 1980s, told me that obedience continued to be one of the incontestable rules in her Catholic family: "When my stepfather was doing these things to me I felt I had no right to say no because he was the boss. When he told me to do something I had to do it — he was the adult and I was the child." For Maya, who grew up at the same time as Jackie, there was a direct connection between her family's "Catholicness," her father's power and the expectation that the children would obey without question:

> I'll give you one little example. It's just a kind of humorous example but here it is. My dad once read or found out somehow that as a father he should lead the grace before supper and also family prayer in the evening. So through my whole childhood he would lead the grace before meals and family prayers and we just had to go along with it. He would even give this explanation of why he was doing it, kind of with this pride in his voice like, "As a father I have

the right to lead the family in prayer." I didn't like it. It made me feel really yucky, like I was being controlled or something. It really felt like a power thing. I mean, he even called it having "the power" to lead prayers. If you think about it, it's kind of sick because a prayer is supposed to be a beautiful thing but it just made me feel really rebellious and angry.

And for Content, the 1970s were the years in which she was sexually abused by one of her older brothers. Her words illustrate in an obvious way that an ideology of male privilege — based not only on gender but also on age — made it difficult to stop her brother's sexual advances:

My brother wasn't mean about it. I just thought that because he was older and I was younger, well, that I had to do it, if that makes sense. I can remember two or three times but I know there were more. It wasn't violent — he'd just come into my room at night. I'd pretend I was asleep and try not to move. I can't remember if he would leave me alone when I pretended to be asleep or if I'd get tired of him pestering me and say to myself, "Oh, just let him get it over with." I'd pretend I was just waking up, and I'd let him do what he had to do and forget about it until the next time. I never told anybody because I thought, "Well, he isn't hurting me — physically anyway." Emotionally, ya, but you don't realize that till you're older. Then you're really screwed up.

The women also told me that their fear of male authority intensified their obedient behaviour. Fear was a by-product of a family ideology in which it was not safe to challenge male power. Cherrie, brought up in a strict Catholic home by adoptive parents during the 1940s and 1950s, trusted her father — until he violated her trust in a profound way:

When I was being abused I was told not to say anything — I was just told to shut up. I guess you could say my father put the fear of God in me. I'd had so much trust in that man. I mean, before [he abused me] I trusted him completely — after that it was trust absolutely nothing. Nothing. Yet I never questioned it. From that day on it was just, "Be a good girl and don't do anything wrong."

Elizabeth said her fear of male authority, established during her late 1930s and 1940s childhood, remained with her into adulthood. Throughout her marriage she suppressed her fear of her husband. But her husband's death in the early 1990s finally enabled her to feel the fear that she had suppressed for decades:

My husband died recently and it was very interesting. It helped me to recognize that I lived in fear all the time when I lived with him. I lived in fear and I didn't even know it — I suppressed it. Suppressed it! He'd never beaten me but there were times when he was sexually inappropriate. But it wasn't even that fear. There was just a total blanket fear, always waiting for that rage to blow and it was frightening to watch. I remember looking at him when he was dead and saying, "I don't ever have to be afraid again. You can never do that to me again." Isn't that amazing?

"GOD THE FATHER"

But the manifestations of male power extended beyond *actual* men in families. "Father God," a powerful form of Catholic imagery used especially during pre–Vatican II times, reinforced men's unchallengeable status in families (recall Cherrie and Faye's words: "My father put the fear of God in me"; "Fathers were supposed to be like God"). Mary Daly argues that the image of "God the Father" is a mechanism of patriarchal ideology that makes the oppression and subordination of women seem natural and fitting.[12] Faye was inundated as a child with the message that the father of the family was to be revered as God was revered:

> The whole idea was that the father of the family, the man of the family or the husband, represented God in the family. I can remember we used to have sermons on those kind of topics regularly, how the man in the family represented God so that you were supposed to have the same attitude towards them that you would have towards God. There was no need to talk about it — it was just the way things were. You obeyed men like you obeyed God. You didn't question them. That was so central to pre–Vatican II Catholicism — this idea that the father represented God's authority in the family and priests represented God's authority in the church. So to question my father would have been like questioning God. It was just unthinkable. And that's not something I thought up, it was taught to us very specifically.

Especially for the women who were abused by their fathers, the impact of patriarchal God imagery was revealed as a painful disjuncture within Catholic family culture. "Father God" imagery widened the existing fault line for these survivors who were already experiencing deep feelings of betrayal and alienation at the hands of their actual fathers. Mary shared this with the group:

> What came out when I was first starting to heal was my anger at God. I was furious. He didn't protect me during that abuse. I was praying — this was a child that knew

every prayer under the sun that Catholics were ever taught, since that's all you ever did was pray — I knew all the prayers in Latin prayer books and all the litanies. So there I was doing the ritual and it wasn't working. He was still abusing me. I'm praying and where's God? Where is he?

Jackie similarly recalled:

There was definitely a point in my healing when I directed my anger toward the church. And that came partly from the fact that every night before I went to bed I would always say my prayers. I always thought of myself as a good kid and I always did the right things and I didn't get in trouble like other kids did. I would ask God to not let the abuse happen anymore. But I didn't use the word "abuse." I asked that he look out for me and not let my stepfather hurt me anymore. And every night it was the same routine. So then I came to the conclusion that there is no God because God loves everybody. But then I thought if God loved me he'd be taking care of me and wouldn't let this happen. I'm not saying I believe that now but that was my take on things for quite a few years.

For Elizabeth, "Father God" imagery compounded her sense of violation:

In my family there was no such thing as privacy. The living conditions were difficult. I didn't have any boundaries ... I had no rights — it wasn't okay to state your needs. There was no sanctity of the person. It took me most of my life to recognize that that's how I felt about Catholicism and God. I felt that my boundaries were being stepped on, *even by God*.

In response, Faye said that as a child she connected the fear of her own father to the fear of "Father God" that was central to her pre–Vatican II upbringing. The fault line again became visible as she described how "Father God" terrified her instead of giving her a sense that she was being protected:

> I still struggle with my relationship with God the father. "Father God" to me, that whole image was a horrifying one. And one that I could never relate to very well. Which makes sense, hey, if you've been abused by your father — it can become a terrifying kind of image.

⁓

As I close this chapter, I am reminded that the official church has only nominally attempted to address the problem of male violence in families. Pope John Paul II has warned Catholics that "a wrong superiority of male prerogatives ... humiliates women and inhibits the development of healthy family relationships."[13] But the question remains: How can it be possible to avoid "a wrong superiority of male prerogatives" within families that retain a traditional, patriarchal structure?

For the eight women in my study, male privilege does not fully explain why they were sexually abused and why it was so difficult for them to challenge their abusers. But for them it is an important piece of the incest puzzle. At the same time, they also stressed that Catholicism was not the only social institution that endorsed male privilege and dominance between the 1940s and 1980s. Yet from their collective standpoint it became clear that Catholicism's salience and influence — especially prior to Vatican II but also during the decades that followed it — shaped gender and sexual relations in profound and indisputable ways. In the next chapters I explore two more pieces of the puzzle: mothering in Catholic families and sexuality.

Chapter 7

CATHOLIC FAMILY IDEOLOGY, MOTHERING AND INCEST

Above all it is important to underline the equal dignity and responsibility of women with men ... The history of salvation, in fact, is a continuous and luminous testimony to the dignity of women ... The true advancement of women requires that clear recognition be given to the value of their maternal and family role, by comparison with all other public roles.[1]   — Pope John Paul II

My mother never came to my protection. None whatsoever. She said nothing. She didn't come to me and say, "Daddy was wrong." As far as I was concerned, Dad was much more important than I was to my mother.

— Cherrie

It would have been very difficult for my mom to leave. Definitely very difficult. She had nowhere to go to. And what would she do with all these kids? It definitely would have been impossible.   — Content

The father was the boss of the house so whatever he would have made me do I did — and my mother perpetuated that idea.   — Mary

I am very upset about the fact that my mother never picked up on the abuse. But I can also understand why she didn't, too. In those days, and the way she kind of reacted towards sex, she wouldn't have picked up anything about the sexual abuse. When people can't handle something, when they feel powerless in a situation, they just don't see it. My mother doesn't believe it ever happened. She doesn't believe incest could ever have happened in our family.
                                                                        — Faye

HAVING EXAMINED CATHOLIC family ideology from the perspective of fathering, I now turn to an exploration of mothering within Catholic families. From the standpoint of the eight women I interviewed, mothering was identified as a deep and painful rupture in their experiences as daughters of Catholic mothers. According to *official* church teachings, the mothers of these eight women should have been able to provide warm, safe and supportive environments for their children. In practice, however, the dominant family ideology left women with few options but to uphold a patriarchal ideology — one that demanded that Catholic wives and mothers give precedence to their marriage vows and the unpaid care of children and home over their own and their children's safety and dignity. The social supports that would have enabled mothers to challenge male power — and take stands in support of their daughters — were simply not in place.

In order to emphasize the significance of the material (that is, socio-economic) conditions of women's lives, I look at the mothers' experiences from a socialist feminist perspective. In doing so I attempt to counter explanations of incest put forward by proponents of *maternal collusion theory.* My aim is *not* to place blame on the shoulders of mothers in incest families. My purpose instead is to highlight the socio-economic contexts that shaped the lives of these mothers, lives in which they made decisions about their own welfare and the welfare of their children.

MOTHERING IN CATHOLIC FAMILIES: OFFICIAL CHURCH TEACHINGS

Catholic family ideology has consistently emphasized the primary importance of women's maternal and domestic role. Catholic mothers are thought of as the guardians of family values and are expected to provide a unifying presence in the family. In 1930, Pope Pius XI reponded to what he considered a strong feminist movement, warning Catholics not to change women's role in the family:

> Many [false teachers] ... assert that ... a subjection of one party to the other is unworthy of human dignity, that the rights of husband and wife are equal; wherefore, they boldly proclaim, the emancipation of women has been or ought to be effected. This emancipation in their ideas must be threefold, in the ruling of the domestic society, in the administration of family affairs and in the rearing of children ... This, however, is not the true emancipation of women, nor that rational exalted liberty which belongs to the noble office of a Christian woman and wife, it is rather the debasing of the womanly character and the dignity of motherhood, and indeed of the whole family.[2]

The 1958 *Catholic Marriage Manual* emphasized that "a woman by nature is generally warm, tender, understanding and loving. These are qualities she should have as mother, homemaker, and custodian of affection and love in the family. Women are not by natural disposition aggressive, authoritative, coldly analytical."[3] And a mother who accepted her role cheerfully was sure to prepare the next generation of women for the "joys of childbearing and childrearing":

> With God's grace, your home is the center of education and of worship. You have the privilege of teaching your children to look at life from a supernatural point of view from an early age, and of encouraging them to accept the facts of life with greater grace. For example, the girl who sees her mother accept motherhood with cheerfulness and love will herself grow up with a proper attitude toward the joys of childbearing and childrearing.[4]

In recent years, Pope John Paul II has also devoted special attention to the role of mothering in Catholic families. By advocating women's natural suitability for domestic, caregiving roles, he continues to support a conservative family model. I quote him here at length:

> Above all it is important to underline the equal dignity and responsibility of women with men ... *The history of salvation, in fact, is a continuous and luminous testimony to the dignity of women* [emphasis added] ... There is no doubt that the equal dignity and responsibility of men and women fully justifies women's access to public functions. On the other hand, *the true advancement of women requires that clear recognition be given to the value of their maternal and family role, by comparison with all other public roles and all other professions* [emphasis added] ... This will come about more easily if ... a renewed "theology of work" can

shed light upon and study in depth the meaning of work in Christian life and determine the fundamental bond between work and the family, and therefore the original and irreplaceable meaning of work in the home be recognized by all in its irreplaceable value ... For possible discrimination between the different types of work and professions is eliminated at its very root once it is clear that all people in every area are working with equal rights and responsibilities ... While it must be recognized that women have the same right as men to perform various public functions, society must be structured in such a way that wives and mothers are not in practice compelled to work outside the home, and that their families can live and prosper in a dignified way even when they themselves devote their full time to their own family. Furthermore, the mentality which honors women more for their work outside the home than for their work within the family must be overcome. This requires that men should truly esteem and love women with total respect for their personal dignity, and that society should create and develop conditions favouring work in the home.[5]

From a feminist perspective, the *formal* claim that women and men are equal within a gendered division of labour is problematic because it ignores men's *de facto* social and economic advantage in families. In other words, it ignores how material conditions mediate the value of unpaid care of children and home and shape everyday/everynight power relations in households.[6] Decades of feminist research and my interviews with incest survivors make it clear that within a capitalist patriarchy women's unpaid domestic and family labour leaves women profoundly vulnerable and does little to promote our "true advancement."

Mothering as a Fault Line in Catholic Family Culture: Attending to Social Context

The practice of mothering in these incestuous families emerged as a clear fault line within Catholic family culture. Catholic family ideology required that "good" Catholic wives and mothers provide precisely the unpaid maternal and emotional labour that left them vulnerable to abuse themselves, dramatically limited their life options and made it difficult for them to support their daughters. The social realities for most of these Catholic mothers — especially those who mothered children before the era of Vatican II and second-wave feminism — included economic dependence, primary responsibility for childcare and domestic labour, a permanent and indissoluble marriage bond, the disavowal of contraception, and in several cases their own histories of incest and sexual abuse. These realities added up to tremendous vulnerability — both for mothers and for daughters. It is within the context of this vulnerability that I account for the mothers' lack of emotional support and denial in the face of their daughters' incest experiences. For mothers, taking a stand against such a profound violation as incest would have been next to impossible without the social and economic supports that would have allowed them to challenge male power in their homes and without an awareness of the signs and significance of incest.

Faye pointed out that the realities of Catholic mothering — the limitations of time, for example — simply did not make it easy for mothers to respond to incest: "Part of what preoccupied a lot of mothers was just having one baby after another — which is part of the Catholic thing. If you look into the reasons why most of them didn't want to know, most of them had their hands full." And, as Faye and Maya reminded us during a group discussion, many mothers had been sexually abused themselves (or at the very least were negatively influenced by Catholic sexual ideology, as discussed in Chapter 8) which seemed to contribute to the mothers' denial and emotional unavailability.

MATERIAL CONDITIONS: SHAPING WOMEN'S CHOICES

During the second focus group discussion we struggled over our explanations for the fact that all eight mothers, in various ways, were emotionally unsupportive and unavailable in the wake of their daughters' distress. We considered the fact that all of the mothers were brought up long before the Vatican II era and second-wave feminism. (Some mothers were brought up in the earliest decades of this century.) We agreed that it is of critical importance to remember that, especially during the earlier decades (the 1940s and 1950s) in which these women were abused, material conditions did not support an emergent awareness of patriarchal families as abusive to women and children. The social supports — day care programs, employment equity initiatives, meaningful full-time employment, to list a few — that would have enabled mothers to challenge male power in their households or seek alternative family arrangements were not in place.[7]

Most mothers would have been unable to seek alternative family arrangements. The women identified several key reasons for their mothers' inability to make a break, all of which were compounded by the dominant Catholic family ideology: economic dependence and the threat of imminent poverty in the wake of marital separation, the threat of alienation from the church in the case of a divorce, enormous domestic responsibilities and large numbers of children to care for, which diminished their ability to earn a living, and illness.

Elizabeth and Faye believe their mothers wanted to leave. Elizabeth said, "I'm sure Mom wanted to leave him many times. But where would she go? How did you do that in those days? Eight kids — what do you do?" Faye emphasized that her mother stayed in the marriage at least in part because she felt it was her duty as a good Catholic wife. "My parents stayed married but they hated one another. They put up with one another until the bitter end. My Mom's favourite saying was, 'You made your bed, you lie in it.' And divorce at that time was a terrible disgrace. You stayed married through thick and thin." Courage told me that her mother tried to leave but ended up returning, mostly for financial reasons.

> Mom left Dad once. We moved back to Nova Scotia because Mom wanted to be closer to her family. She had no family in Ontario. So we were in Halifax for about six months. My dad always made good money and he'd send us money plus she was getting social assistance but it wasn't very much. The homes we lived in in Ontario were always nice and she wasn't used to living in a rat-trap apartment. So after six months we went back.

Maya believes her mother would have left sooner had she been economically independent from the beginning: "She might not have put up with Dad for so long." Content, whose mother had twelve children and a terminal illness, told me: "It would have been very difficult for my mom to leave. Definitely very difficult. She had nowhere to go to. And what would she do with all these kids? It definitely would have been impossible." The disjuncture between her mother's experience and Catholicism's staunch stand against contraception was obvious:

> My mother wasn't supposed to have that many kids because she was sick. She ended up having twelve children. After

she was diagnosed with cancer, she was told she wasn't supposed to have that many kids but she kept having them. She wasn't allowed to use contraceptives. I think it distressed her a lot [to have that many children]. The more kids she had the longer it took her to recover from her illness. Maybe if she hadn't had so many kids she wouldn't have gotten as sick and it wouldn't have taken her as long to recover [after each pregnancy].

Mary compared her mother's situation with her own, giving weight to the notion that an awareness of ruptures in women's lives emerges when the material conditions are right. When it came time for Mary to work through her memories of abuse, she had a safe and supportive environment — something her mother had never had:

Mothers were isolated. They had their everyday work world and they had to keep quiet because what other woman was going to share that trash with them? They would have thought they were the only one in the world, likely. When I started to remember the abuse we had our women's centre and I trusted some women and I started talking, little by little. My mother would never have had that. There was no women's group where they could talk and learn to trust.

Cherrie defended her mother by saying, "I don't think mothers had the knowledge of what to look for. Who at that time would have been aware of sexual abuse?" And in response Faye reminded us that sexual abuse has only recently come into wide public awareness:

We're in a different cultural atmosphere now. There's a lot more publicity. Even ten years ago we thought incest was rare, so if anybody had faced the fact that there was incest in their family they would have been immediately stigmatized. And they wouldn't have had any support, or they certainly wouldn't have expected anyone else to relate to them ... All I have to do is think back twenty years ago when I was working as a psychologist and we never picked it up. There we were with people in front of us trying to understand why people were behaving the way they were. I didn't pick it up and I was trained as a psychologist *and* I was an incest survivor!

Three of the women told me their mothers denied obvious signs that the incest was happening and did not support their daughters' efforts to stop the incest. The others said their mothers were not attentive to the signs of their distress and were unable to provide the protection needed to put a stop to the abuse. Far from being "warm, tender, understanding and loving,"[8] as Kelly's *Catholic Marriage Manual* expected Catholic mothers to be, Faye's mother was emotionally cold and distant:

> My mother was a very cold person emotionally. She was hopeless as far as any kind of emotional contact ... I don't ever remember telling my mother about the incest. It was partly because of the alienation and emotional distance between us. She just wasn't the person I would go to. If I could go back and change the way things were I would have made my mother different so that she wasn't so emotionally detached from her children. It would've made a big difference in my life if I'd felt closer to my mother, if she'd been more approachable and more open to hearing about my distress. But she wasn't.

Jackie was sexually abused by her stepfather for many years. Although in the earliest interview she emphasized her mother's lack of support, in a later interview she recalled: "I think on some level my mother knew that something was definitely wrong. But I think she was scared herself and she didn't really know what to do." That Jackie's mother was employed outside the home undoubtedly helped her leave a marriage with a man who was clearly abusing her daughter physically and emotionally, if not also sexually.

Among Cherrie's recollected memories of abuse is a memory of her mother actually witnessing an episode of the incest between Cherrie and her father. The event Cherrie described occurred during the late 1940s:

Dad was a big man, six feet tall and two hundred pounds. Strong as a bull. So it was normal that you'd do what he told you to. I think the abuse put fear into me right from the beginning. The two flashbacks I have of my dad I was about the same age. In one I was in Mom and Dad's bedroom and he had my skirt up and his pants down. Mom walked in and saw us but she turned right back around and went out. I never saw such a disgusted look on her face. I felt she was disgusted with me. He told me he was doing this because I was a bad girl, because I'd done something wrong. I don't know if Dad knew Mom walked in. But I think he noticed the look on my face because he got up quickly and put me on the floor. He pulled up his pants, walked out and left me there sitting on the floor. I just sat there and cried and cried. My mother never came to my protection. None whatsoever. She said nothing. She didn't come to me and say, "Daddy was wrong." As far as I was concerned, Dad was much more important than I was to my mother. She wasn't about to kick him out of the house. Why would she kick him out just because of me? As far as the church goes, you're supposed to turn the other cheek, forgive and forget. And I'm sure she would've been afraid of him too if she had said something to him.

She wasn't the type to burst out in anger at him. It was like, well I'm married to him and he's my husband and that's Michael. Don't you dare say anything negative about him. She was very protective of him and very supportive of him, and therefore he was number one in her life. And hey, as an adopted child, I was just a drop-in.

If we look at this encounter within the social context of Cherrie's Catholic family we must recognize that a woman taking a stand against her own husband would have fundamentally challenged his power in the home. The difficulty in challenging male power would certainly have been intense prior to the 1960s when there was a widespread acceptance that fathers were the "head of the household" and little feminist consciousness about family violence. And in not challenging her husband, Cherrie's mother may have been preventing violence being used against her as well ("I'm sure she would've been afraid of him too if she had said something"). Perhaps most important was the fact that Cherrie's mother relied on her husband for financial support — and it would not have been in her interest to threaten the source of her own, and her children's, economic security. If we take into account how this complex (and undoubtedly incomplete) set of social conditions may have influenced this mother's decision not to challenge her husband, we can better understand Dorothy Smith's claim that material conditions affect the historical moments at which the ruptures in women's experience emerge.

CATHOLIC MOTHERING: A QUESTION OF IDENTITY

But the mothers' socio-economic vulnerability may not have been the only factor influencing their decisions to stay. These mothers had a lot invested in their identities and acted out of their socially reinforced roles as Catholic wives and mothers. Catholicism's "honour and shame" code esteemed wives and mothers for their selflessness, sexual purity and devotion to their husbands and family. It was this honour and shame code that subtly controlled women. Faye recalled:

> My father was a very domineering man, very controlling. He really had high expectations. He wouldn't ask my mother for a cup of tea. He'd just say, "Cup of tea, Kath." And that was the way he treated her — like she was there to kind of cater to him. She just accepted it. Women were supposed to put the man at the centre of their lives.

Faye also suggested that in the Irish Catholic community in which she was raised, the Catholic family ideology esteemed women for staying in a marriage so that their identities as Catholic wives often took precedence over their own and their children's physical safety. If there was violence in the family, women simply lived with it:

> I grew up in a very violent culture. On Saturday nights our idea of entertainment was to stand on our back porches and watch the domestic violence — wives and furniture and children being sent through the windows when the men would come home drunk from the pubs. But wives were always expected to stay with their husbands. I mean, it was far worse to not have a husband than to have a husband who beat you up. So I think the biggest thing keeping women in marriages was that in those days divorce was such an incredible disgrace — especially in that Catholic

community. It was just unthinkable to get divorced. You would have been ostracized, shunned in the community. My mother would never have allowed that to happen to us. Women were really trapped in those days, not just financially, but by the whole culture.

Mary said that although her mother was esteemed as a pillar of Catholic womanhood in their Cape Breton community, she didn't provide the care and support that Mary needed:

> I may have felt that my mother would never believe me if I told her [about the incest]. Now I'm not sure, I may have told her in my own way and she didn't believe or didn't listen. I would be scared to tell her even now, if she were still living, in case she wouldn't believe me. It's still quite a thing. My mother was more like the church was — unapproachable. She tried to be a role model. I almost analyse her like the Blessed Virgin. She was the pure part of our family, untouchable.

That Catholic women were to model themselves on the Virgin Mary may have been a nearly universal phenomenon during those decades. Faye, who grew up in England far away from Mary's Cape Breton community, recalled:

> I know that when I was growing up the ideal woman would model herself on Mary. Mary was seen as a very submissive figure: "Let it be done unto me according to your will." And that was supposed to be transferred to the mother. We were taught that directly by the nuns. Mary was our model, especially as a wife and a mother. And it was a very distorted picture of Mary because they taught us that she was completely subservient to God and therefore completely subservient to her husband. So it was a

very direct teaching. And the role of women, all the women I knew, modelled themselves on Mary. She was seen as the ideal.

A supportive response to incest, then, would have challenged male power in the family and placed them directly at odds with the dictates of their identities as "good" Catholic wives and mothers.

MOTHERS' OWN HISTORIES OF SEXUAL ABUSE

A compounding factor in the mothers' denial and failure to protect seemed to be the intergenerational patterns of incest and sexual abuse. Several of the women said their mothers' own histories of sexual abuse made it difficult for them to respond. Maya illustrated this point:

> My mother is also a survivor of childhood sexual abuse. And I think she's wondering why as a survivor herself she wouldn't have recognized that the same thing was happening to her daughter. She doesn't want to look at it. She didn't want to tell me anything further, any other details. I think she really needs to look at this. I think she thinks it's such a big, overwhelming thing that she'd rather keep a lid on it than explore it. But I think this asexuality thing, the thing where my parents seemed pretty asexual and how it affected me not being able to think about or talk about sexuality, I think a lot of that might come from her bad experiences as a child. I think she has a real blind spot. Like whatever part of her soul that's supposed to be a sexual woman is not functioning. That energy is being taken up by other things — her work, her role as a mother, her role as a religious person.

Faye suspects that her mother was sexually abused. "My mother certainly hasn't admitted to it but given how I saw her act with certain family members, I'd be willing to bet she was." When I asked her if her mother was aware of the incest between Faye and her father she explained:

> You see, if she'd been abused herself and repressed all that then she just wouldn't have been able to see it, because anything sexual would've immediately been kind of denied. You could never say anything about sex to my mother. Well, I mean, I can talk to her now. But when we were younger she was very strait-laced, I guess, in that sense. We could never say a dirty joke in front of her. She was very, very uptight about sex. Again it was part of the Catholic thing which would have made it very difficult to tell her what was going on. For one thing, because we never knew anything about sex I didn't even have the words for what was going on. And, another thing, because I knew that my mother just reacted so negatively and was so horrified by anything sexual it just would've been hopeless. I don't remember ever trying to tell her. Looking back now, I can see why I wouldn't have. Partly because sex wasn't talked about and partly because we had this really distant relationship. I wasn't close to her at all — emotionally she was very cut off.

Today Faye feels resolved (although still deeply unhappy) about her mother's lack of support because she now understands that mothering within such a strongly anti-sexual climate prevented women from developing a critical consciousness. Without a critical awareness of her own sexuality and possible history of abuse, it would have been next to impossible for Faye's mother to see the sexual abuse of her daughter:

I am very upset about the fact that my mother never picked up on the abuse. But I can also understand why she didn't, too ... In those days, and the way she kind of reacted towards sex, she wouldn't have picked up on anything sexual. When people can't handle something, when they feel powerless in a situation, they just don't see it. So I don't think she would have had any way of handling [the incest] and she just wouldn't have seen it.

Elizabeth's denial of her own children's sexual abuse helps us understand how the process of denial can happen:

The whole thing [about my children having been sexually abused] came out when the second youngest started to have serious marriage problems. You assume you hear everything your children tell you, but several years before he started to have the marriage problems he disclosed to me about the abuse. It was at the time that I was disclosing to him about my own abuse and I guess I was so into my own abuse at the time that I didn't even hear him. So I didn't do anything about it. I might've been in shock about it. So I heard about it again when he started to have marital problems. It's amazing what the human mind can do — repress memories and information when you have to, especially if you haven't dealt with your own abuse or you're in the middle of dealing with your own. I can understand a parent who reacts this way because I've done it myself. I don't think I would've reacted that way if I hadn't been abused myself. The first time I didn't deal with it because I was just barely touching base with mine and I didn't know how to respond. I went numb, absolutely numb. Something inside of me just stopped. It was like, "I can't deal with this." So I did my old dissociating trick, and I didn't. Just pulled it off beautifully. I think it's very real that we don't see something like this right away ... It's the most shocking thing you can hear your child say. It's just so unfathomable that anyone could do this to your child. So when my son came back in distress two or three years after the first time he told me, that's when it started to come through. By that time I had worked enough on my own abuse to be able to recognize what he was saying to me, and that it was something that had to be dealt with.

And Mary's daughter is also a survivor of incest:

I guess I should have known in the case of my own daughter. I just thought she had a behavioural problem. I think I didn't want to know. So when you're looking at mothers who didn't have any of that kind of training [awareness about incest and sexual abuse] I don't know how you could ever have expected them to respond to their children. And a lot of those mothers had training to suppress because they were abused themselves. In many ways my daughter repeated my pattern. It breaks my heart that it couldn't have been prevented.

∾

In these eight families, then, the women identified mothering as another critical piece of the incest puzzle. The combined realities of male privilege (as we saw in Chapter 6) and the mothers' vulnerability clearly suggest that Catholic family ideology and its concomitant practices fostered incestuous sexual abuse (as well as other forms of family violence). In recent decades, with the push toward secularism and the increase in women's opportunities to work outside the home, the context of mothering in Catholic families has undoubtedly undergone a transition. At the same time, we are faced with the insistence from the official Catholic church that mothers return to their "proper" place in the home. But the accounts of these women's lives as daughters of Catholic mothers illustrate unequivocally the disjuncture — the line of fault — between the *idealized* role for Catholic mothers (at bottom, one of selflessness and economic dependence) and the *realities* for mothers and daughters in traditional Catholic families. In the following chapter, I explore with these eight women a third piece of the puzzle: Catholic sexual ideology and its implications for incest survivors.

Chapter 8

INCEST AND CATHOLIC SEXUAL IDEOLOGY

Christian revelation recognizes two specific ways of realizing the vocation of the human person, in its entirety, to love: marriage and virginity or celibacy. Either one is in its own proper form an actuation of the most profound truth of man [sic], of his being "created in the image of God" ... The only "place" in which the self-giving in its whole truth [that is, sexual intercourse] is made possible is marriage.[1]
— Pope John Paul II

∾

When I was growing up, even within marriage sex was considered sinful. It wasn't considered a mortal sin to have sex within marriage but it was [at least considered] a venial sin. Today I still occasionally hear the older Catholics talking about that. You weren't supposed to have sex for pleasure. Period. It was only for procreation. Because of that all sex was secret — not just abusive sex — any kind of sex was just horrendous. — Faye

I guess there was no model, no precedent for talking about anything about sexuality. Think of trying to talk to someone about outer space travel, something they never would

have done or experienced and try to talk to them about it.
You don't even have the language, really.   — Maya

There must have been pages if you lined up all our rules
[about sex] ... There's no way there's enough time to convey the guilt they [parents, nuns and priests] were able to
put on us.   — Mary

I remember the heavy guilt feeling I had as a child. During
the Lenten days we always had to do some little penance
to purify ourselves. And I remember a desperate need to
really purge myself, to purify myself because I felt dirty. So
I tied a knotted belt around my waist and imitated the old
stories of the saints that you'd hear. To me, that was the
way that I could be pure, that I could be okay.
                                        — Elizabeth

IT'S COMMON knowledge that sexuality has never been a neutral subject for Catholics. Over the centuries, the official
Catholic church has consistently held that sexuality is morally
allowable in one forum alone: heterosexual, monogamous, indissoluble marriage. Historically, then, sexual activity was denied or strongly discouraged among Catholics who were
unmarried, lesbian, gay, divorced or members of a religious
order. In a 1981 document, Pope John Paul II summarized
the official position on sexuality:

> Christian revelation recognizes two specific ways of realizing
> the vocation of the human person, in its entirety, to love:
> marriage and virginity or celibacy. Either one is in its own
> proper form an actuation of the most profound truth of
> man [sic], of his being "created in the image of God"...The
> only "place" in which the self-giving in its whole truth [that
> is, sexual intercourse] is made possible is marriage.[2]

This "sex-only-within-marriage" tenet shaped Catholic family culture by laying the groundwork for a strictly regulated "honour and shame code."[3] It was reinforced by:

1. a plethora of rules that rewarded sexual purity/restraint and punished sexual "impropriety,"

2. threats of abandonment by the church or one's family/community for transgressions of the code,

3. church sacraments and rituals (especially prior to Vatican II) such as Holy Communion, which demanded sexual purity, and confession, which functioned as the way to purify oneself from impious sexual acts and thoughts,

4. the threat of spending an eternity in hell for committing sins of a sexual nature,

5. priests and nuns in the institutional church and parochial schools who were granted exceptional authority on sexual matters,

6. the promotion of celibacy and the religious life as a superior vocation, and

7. "Father God" imagery that reinforced the rightness of Catholicism's rigid and punitive stance on sexuality.

In this chapter I explore painful points of disjuncture between the church's *official* position on sexuality and eight women's *actual* experiences of sexuality, including their experiences of incest, in Catholic families. Doing so exposes the church's official position on sexuality as an *ideological* one — a position that has strengthened men's domination over women and children and helped to alienate women from their actual everyday/everynight experiences. I also make links between Catholic *sexual* ideology and Catholic *family* ideology as complementary — not competing — tenets of Catholic patriarchal ideology. These tenets, which conflate womanhood primarily with sexuality and fertility, provided the justification for controlling and "domesticating" women within the private sphere of the family. This, in turn, contributed to conditions that stifled women's autonomy and intellectual development, and fostered many forms of violation.[4]

CATHOLIC SEXUAL IDEOLOGY: POINTS OF DISJUNCTURE IN EIGHT WOMEN'S LIVES

The dominant forms of consciousness in each of these incest families were strongly shaped by shame, denial and fear of sexuality (what Carter Heyward calls "erotophobia"[5]) and the belief that sex outside of marriage is, quite simply, a very, very bad thing. For the women brought up prior to the 1960s, Catholicism was particularly rigid and damaging. Mary emphasized: "There must have been pages if you lined up all our rules [about sex] ... There's no way there's enough time to convey the guilt they [parents, nuns and priests] were able to put on us." And even though Catholicism's rigidity about sexuality softened somewhat following Vatican II, the four women born during the 1960s were still significantly influenced by parents, priests, nuns and teachers who had themselves been "schooled" in pre–Vatican II Catholicism.

As incest survivors, these women (as children) were not willing partners in sexual acts — they were forced. Yet within the Catholic family culture of the time, these sexual acts amounted to a fundamental breach of Catholicism's honour and shame code. As very young Catholic girls who were "sexually active," they internalized the message that they were sexually impure. As girls growing up within an overall Catholic culture that fostered notions of women's morally inferior status, they found it easy to think of themselves as "evil" and "irredeemable." And as girls who were growing up within staunchly Catholic families where there was next to no awareness about incest as a form of *abusive, non-consensual* sex, they learned to cope with profound sexual violations by blaming and punishing themselves. As a result, their feelings of self-worth suffered in almost indescribable ways. Moreover, the guilt and psychological weight of having "broken" Catholicism's fundamental rule about sexuality dramatically undermined their efforts to seek protection from further abuse.

Sexual Purity, Sexual Shame

In the decades preceding Vatican II (as in other times in the Catholic church's history), Catholics considered sexual sins to be among the most serious. Catholics distinguished between two types of sin. A "mortal sin," the more grave of the two types, was thought to be an act committed against God, freely and with a person's complete knowledge. In contrast, "venial sins" were not wholly voluntary and were thought not to violate God's will in a "fundamental" way.[6] Again, it is important to remember that the lack of awareness about incest as a form of enforced, non-consensual sexual activity meant that, in practice, these survivors internalized the incest as something for which they *were* wholly responsible. Despite the fact that they weren't responsible for it, several of the survivors believed the incest placed them in a state of mortal sin. This had profound repercussions for their self-esteem and their fears of a future of having to "reckon with God."

Mary provided one of the most powerful and clearest examples. In the following excerpt we can see how a priest's

response to her disclosure reflected the overall lack of consciousness (it was the early 1950s, after all) about sexual
abuse as a social phenomenon and, relatedly, a perpetrator's
— not a victim's — culpability in a case of sexual abuse. The
Catholic emphasis on sexual purity and individual account-
ability for sin, alongside an impossible expectation that Mary
put a stop to her father's sexual advances, clearly illustrates a
disjuncture within her experience of Catholic culture:

> Growing up, we had this nun in school who used to ask
> us, the boys really, what we were going to be when we
> grew up. And they'd all stick up their hands and say,
> "Priests." And all the girls would put up their hands and
> say, "Sisters." They knew what she would want to hear and
> a lot of people did take up [religious] vocations in those
> days. But I was one of the ones who would never put my
> hand up. I know now, in retrospect, it was probably be-
> cause I didn't feel worthy. That was really sad, because that
> stuck with me all my life, that feeling of not being worthy.
> So when it came time to prepare for First Communion I
> was one of those rebels who would give Sister a hard time.
> I wouldn't partake in the ritual, I wasn't cooperative and
> she just couldn't understand it. So she called my mother
> and my mother, for some reason right off the bat, got the
> priest to come to my home and speak to me. So this priest
> came in to talk to me and sat me on his lap and talked to
> me about Communion. And this is when I disclosed for
> the first time. I told him, "My daddy and me do bad
> things together." I was trying to explain why I couldn't
> take Communion. And he told me that would not happen
> any more, that I mustn't let it happen, that I was forgiven.
> Well, that was fine for that occasion. But then once I took
> First Communion he was wrong, it did happen again.
> Only this time I went to the priest and told him I let it

happen again and then I was twice as bad. So it was really a bad background. Later when I stopped confessing it to the priest I was reinforcing [the badness] because every time I went to confession I was omitting a big sin because it happened over and over. And what's worse, I went to Communion with that sin on my soul.

For Mary's history of incest, then, confession, and the sacrament of Holy Communion had significant implications. Mary continued:

Of course, those were the days when you ran to confession every week. I remember the agony over having kissed a boy very thoroughly and thinking it was *so* wrong. I was, oh, I don't know, fourteen. Having to go to confession over that was such agony ... If you didn't go to confession every week you were giving scandal and if you didn't receive Communion you were giving scandal because it meant you were in [a state of] mortal sin. It had something to do with being that holy vessel, you know, not taking in the host in an unclean body ... And as a survivor that hadn't disclosed that she'd sucked her dad's penis that day or that she'd slept with him that night or whatever, if you didn't disclose that in confession and you turned around and had Communion the next day you were doubly dirty, your soul was totally black. God help you if you died before you confessed because where were you going to go? Straight to hell!

Every one of the eight women talked about ways in which the Catholic culture of that era emphasized sexual restraint and purity. They also talked about the shame and punishment associated with failing to be sexually pure. Faye told me that during the 1940s and 1950s, *any* kind of sex was thought to be a sin:

I was brought up in the Irish Catholic community in Liverpool, which was a very oppressive kind of Catholicism. You know, rigid, legalistic, lots of guilt. And when I was growing up, even within marriage sex was considered sinful. It wasn't considered a mortal sin to have sex within marriage but it was [at least considered] a venial sin. Today I still occasionally hear the older Catholics talking about that. You weren't supposed to have sex for pleasure. Period. It was only for procreation. Because of that all sex was secret — not just abusive sex. Any kind of sex was just horrendous.

Shame about sexuality was clearly part of the Catholic culture in Mary's rural Cape Breton community:

One of the biggest things I remember is shame [about sexuality]. Like when my period began at the age of ten [my mother told me] I wasn't even allowed to tell my best friend. It was too shameful. I was just passed a box of Kotex and told, "Never, never leave a dirty one around where your brothers or father will see it."... I went through so much of my life being ashamed of my body and I had a normal body. I know that in retrospect but I didn't grow up feeling that way. I'm no longer ashamed of my body — but I definitely blame our church for an awful lot of that body shame.

The interviews also revealed that Catholics went to great lengths to avoid the shame associated with transgressing the sexual code. In the late 1960s, Content's older sister had an unplanned pregnancy and was forced by her parents to marry the father of her child — a man who was known in the community as a violent alcoholic. Clearly the focus was more on the shame that pregnancy out of wedlock would bring upon the family than the dignity and safety of this unmarried mother-to-be. After twenty-five years, Content's sister finally left her violent marriage:

> Now it's twenty-five years down the road and she just left him now, three kids later, she left him. He was beating her then and that was known at the time that she married him. He had a drinking problem, too, and he was drinking a lot at the time. But my parents, and my mother's side of the family especially, felt strongly that she had to get married because of the shame [a pregnancy outside of marriage] would bring to the family.

It is clear, then, that Catholicism's honour and shame code about sexuality had particularly acute implications for girls and women. These implications were due, in part, to the fact that Catholic women were rewarded and esteemed for sexual purity and marital fidelity — for these were qualities in women that ensured the integrity and survival of "the Catholic family." The implications were also due to the dominant forms of consciousness within Catholic family culture that placed a special burden on women: warding off the label of "sexual temptress." So when women in these incest families (especially mothers and grandmothers) upheld Catholic sexual ideology in such a forceful way, there were ramifications for these incest survivors. Maya told me the beliefs held by the women in her family affected the way she dealt with her abuse:

> In my family I learned that it was the woman's responsibility to "avoid occasions of sin" and that if something sexual happened, the woman was the one to blame ... I remember once my grandmother saw one of my sisters holding hands with her boyfriend. She gave her this huge lecture about being too young to hold hands with a boy. She said, "You're only nineteen. You're too young to be holding

hands with a boy. If you're engaged to be married, well, maybe then." My mother [this grandmother's daughter] upholds the belief of all the women in my family — that men can't help themselves so women have to be responsible for controlling sex. It's a sort of pre–Vatican II belief that women are supposed to control their sexuality and men can't help themselves, they're just slaves to their hormones. Therefore women with their cooler heads and supposedly less strong drives are the ones that are supposed to be on guard and responsible and make sure nothing sexual happens. And there was also this "give an inch they'll take a mile" kind of idea. It's funny how these lessons came down through the women. It prevented me from telling anybody for years — even from being able to say it to myself.

Elizabeth, whose mother, like Maya's grandmother, was brought up in the earliest decades of the twentieth century, recollected:

It was my mother who behaved dysfunctionally sexually. She's the one who taught us to hate our bodies ... When I think of the Catholic church and the values we were brought up with I have a hard time connecting my father to those values. It was really my mother who was the tyrant ... I remember one time I was out with a fellow. I was young, oh, maybe thirteen or fourteen. It was about eight o'clock on a summer night and he was just holding my hand. But when my mother saw us she flew into a rage. There was a fear in her, a panic in her that makes you suspicious when you look at it now.

Jackie told me that no one in her family was comfortable talking about sex, but she identified her mother as especially rigid when it came to sexuality:

There was a lot of shame about sex. I guess it was weird because although it wasn't talked about there were under-lying messages — that it shouldn't be talked about, that it was dirty and cheap ... I remember going to a party once with some friends and there was a guy there that I really liked. I remember he gave me a hickey that night and the next day my Mom looked at me and knew what it was. I felt so low and trashy and cheap because she made me feel like it was the worst thing I could have done.

It is perhaps no wonder that, in this family culture, Jackie de-cided not to disclose the incest to her mother.

SECRECY AND SILENCE

For these women, secrecy and silence about sexuality also contributed to their inability to name the abuse and to ask non-abusing parents and care-givers for protection. Accord-ing to Dorothy Smith, ruling ideology (in this case, Catholic sexual ideology) depends upon and takes for granted the si-lences of those who do not benefit from ruling relations.[7] Faye noted that the aspect of Catholic culture most support-ing the incest was this tendency toward secrecy: "Growing up in a Catholic culture, which I did, the values and beliefs of that culture really supported the secrecy more than anything else about the incest." (Recall that Faye also said: "You weren't supposed to have sex for pleasure. Period. It was only for pro-creation. Because of that all sex was secret — not just abusive sex.") Mary agreed with Faye: "I despise secrets. If I could eliminate anything in a child's life it would be the necessity of having secrets."

In Maya's home, the way sexuality was handled was to

simply deny it altogether. This silenced her when she was looking for ways to stop the incest with her uncle:

> I think I had an idea that what was going on with my uncle was something embarrassing to talk about, like any type of sexuality or couples' thing was kind of just not talked about. Probably partly because my parents didn't have a really good relationship I think I had the idea that any kind of sexuality wasn't something that I was expected to have or people in my family weren't supposed to have or show or do. It would have been too threatening for my family to see me as a sexual person. So that was a seed in myself that never sprouted. They didn't have to kill it, it didn't even sprout! The positive reinforcement I got when I was growing up seemed always to be based on one main thing and that was my intelligence and how well I did at school. Now I find that my self-worth is built upon too small a foundation ... One thing I've learned is how this whole thing was really hidden and underhanded. Like, with Cecil, we were both acting in a manipulating, under-handed way, neither of us was, you know, in your face about it. It would've been totally the opposite if say Cecil had come up during broad daylight, lifted up my skirt and tried to fondle me and I punched him in the face. That would've been him acting openly and me responding openly but it was totally the opposite ... I tried to explain what was happening to my mother. I was trying to give her some idea of what was going on but I wasn't able to frame it in terms of me being a victim. I was trying to say, "We're more than friends" or "Something is going on with us." But she didn't pick up any clues as to any unhealthiness that was going on. So I guess there was no model, no precedent for talking about anything about sexuality. Think of trying to talk to someone about outer space

travel, something they never would have done or experienced and try to talk to them about it. You don't even have the language really ... The fact that I wasn't identifying the abuse for so many years is probably in large part because the ideology was so heavy and so prevalent in our particular family. This culture of asexuality, it's part of this whole church ideology because of that attitude that people aren't really sexual and if they are you certainly shouldn't hear about it. Because of that I was silenced.

Elizabeth described how she knew intuitively that the way her father was treating her wasn't right but that she didn't have the correct words to help her stop her father's sexual violations. Since she was abused during the 1940s and 1950s, it's not surprising that other family members also lacked the language to help her put a stop to them:

> I would have told you long before I remembered [the incest with my dad] how I used to get annoyed at my father for always feeling my ass and yet it didn't connect that he was violating me ... I wouldn't have known to call it violating me then at all. I just knew, "It's not okay for you to do that to me — it doesn't feel right." I told him to stop. My mother told him to stop. But it was never recognized as a violation. It really wasn't. And yet it was recognized as not right.

Language was not only lacking about incest. In some cases, basic information about sexuality wasn't available either, even into the 1970s and 1980s. Content told me about her years of anguish over believing that her brother's fondling could have made her pregnant:

> As a teenager when I was going through puberty I developed this tiny little pot belly and I kept thinking I was pregnant. It sounds silly but we didn't have much education

then and I think it was when I was about in junior high that they started teaching it. I thought that whatever my brother was doing with me — just fondling really — could have made me pregnant. And I thought that even if it had happened three years ago it could still be catching up with me now! I wondered, months were going by, why wasn't I getting more pregnant? I had no idea what my period had to do with pregnancy.

SUFFERING AND THE "MARTYR SYNDROME"

Feminist researchers have previously made links between the Christian "virtue" of suffering and childhood sexual abuse. Sheila Redmond, for example, states that "the justification or honouring of suffering can have a negative impact on the victims of child sexual abuse ... [because] martyrdom is an extreme form of suffering [yet] holds a special place of honour with the Christian tradition."[8] The women I interviewed concurred with this viewpoint. As a child, Mary was encouraged to silently "offer up" her pain and suffering. Being rewarded for keeping silent in the face of suffering therefore compounded Mary's silence about the incest:

> You got an extra indulgence if you offered up your pain and sadness. Or if you wanted something and didn't get it you offered that up for the souls in purgatory. "Offer it up," we used to say. The only thing is it wouldn't count if you talked about it. You had to keep it private. Martyrs, that's what we were. I call it the martyr syndrome!

It's no wonder that by her late teens, after many years of being forced into sex with her father, Mary felt profoundly unworthy. She had "failed" to live up to the expectations placed on "good Catholic girls." So when she was sexually violated by other men — a school principal and, later, a boyfriend — she believed it was punishment she deserved:

> It was no time till I met some other guy who was going to take advantage of me. Ironically, I disclosed to him that I'd been raped [by a school principal] and that was what cut me off. And, of course, at that time I had no conscious memories of the abuse with my father. Like I had no feelings, sexuality feelings, I felt completely neutral. And so he was going to prove to me that I could feel. It was really like date rape. He'd give me drinks and then just do it. And it would be horrible and it would be painful and emotionally disgusting. *But I thought I deserved the punishment. I was convinced.* The whole ordeal was a punishment. It was painful, there was no pleasure to it but it was what I deserved as a young Catholic who'd had sex with her father, drank too much, run away from home, left her siblings abandoned, you name it. I could list a half dozen reasons — it'd be a matter of choice which one you picked.

Elizabeth told us that her first experience of sexual abuse led to a "desperate need" to purify herself. She linked this to her sense of guilt about the sexual abuse and to what she had learned in her Catholic upbringing about suffering and penance:

> At the age of four I was very badly abused and not long after that — this might sound utterly ridiculous but a child of about five or six had this desperate need to purge, to be pure, to get clean. I remember the heavy guilt feeling I had as a child. During the Lenten days we always had to do some little penance to purify ourselves. And I remember a desperate need to really purge myself, to purify myself because I felt dirty. So I tied a knotted belt around my

waist and imitated the old stories of the saints that you'd hear. To me, that was the way that I could be pure, that I could be okay.

CATHOLICISM AND EXPERIENCES OF SEXUALITY

As I listened to these women during the course of our many interviews, incest wasn't the only kind of painful sexual experience they described. In a variety of ways, the practices and attitudes arising out of Catholic sexual ideology impeded women's ability to establish meaningful, mutual sexual relationships and stifled positive feelings about their bodies. Mary told me:

> Every time I had to have intercourse I cried and I was very good at hiding it because I knew it wouldn't do very much for [my husband's] ego. You know, good Catholics have intercourse in the dark, so he wouldn't have ever known how I felt! [Intercourse] just felt so dirty and unwanted. It was a very one-sided affair — man-in and man-out. To be fair to him he was young and green and knew nothing about lovemaking and he was just doing his best. He was against an obstacle and a half, there's no two ways about it. So it's no wonder the first fifteen years of our marriage were hell ... I think if there was a way that I was gypped in my life, the biggest way, it was with my sexual fulfilment ... Certainly the Catholic heritage stifled an awful lot of spiritual growth because in the past we were so into being ashamed of even feeling normal feelings. I know there was a day as a teenager when I had normal sexual feelings — but running to confession the very next day about it! Put that in perspective, eh? "Put those feelings away! Say penance and do some acts of holy charity!" Holy frig! You know, with

that kind of repetition it was almost brainwashing. I went through so much of my life being ashamed of my body and I had a normal body. I know that in retrospect, but I didn't grow up feeling that. I am no longer ashamed of my body but I definitely blame our church for an awful lot of that body shame.

Courage believes that an absence of sexual pleasure and even marital rape were commonplace in her mother's everyday/everynight life. Her words are a reminder that marriage (for Catholics, the only morally allowable sexual relationship) is no guarantee of a dignified existence for women:

One night my mom's sister was talking about sex, saying something about an orgasm, and my mother said, "What's an orgasm?" I said, "Oh, my God, Mom! You've never had an orgasm?" She was getting sort of angry because we were all talking and laughing and she didn't know what we were talking about. She said, "Well, you know what your father was like. He'd get drunk, jump into bed, do it, fart and roll over." I think for her it was almost like being raped most times. A couple of times I'm sure he did rape her because I remember her crying and telling him to get off of her and stuff. I think if my mom didn't have such strong denial she would have cracked up by now.

From Elizabeth's standpoint, the Catholic church's endorsement of male dominance has made it easy to slip into incest but it has also supported other sexual violations such as marital rape.

When it comes to incest and the church, we know that the role of the men has been taught as the dominant and powerful one and that it's been very easy to slip into incest because the church has almost given men a carte blanche.

They weren't saying, "You have a right to go and sexually abuse," but they were saying, "You have a right." Like when you get married your wife is supposed to fulfil all your needs. It's your *right* as a husband to expect this. That's not teaching men mutuality and respect. That's teaching them dominance.

∾

Clearly, then, beliefs and practices relating to sexuality within these Catholic families have been identified as yet another piece of the incest puzzle. All eight incest survivors recalled that, as young girls, they were forced to deal with the pain of a stolen sexual innocence and profound loss of control over their own lives. But at the same time they were forced to bear the weight of a secretive, punitive and shame-based sexual culture. In other words, Catholic sexual ideology compounded their experiences of incest in significant ways.

If we examine carefully the points of disjuncture within these women's everyday/everynight lives, we can begin to make links between incest and other ways in which women have been sexually controlled and violated within Catholic family culture. This, in turn, may bring us to question and ultimately reject one of Catholicism's basic beliefs: that sex is morally appropriate *only* within a sanctified, lifelong and heterosexual marriage. For although the Catholic church has upheld this belief in the name of "safeguarding the family," girls and women have paid far too high a price.

Chapter 9

HEALING THE POINTS OF RUPTURE IN CATHOLIC FAMILIES

At a moment in history in which the family is the object of numerous forces that seek to destroy it or in some way to deform it, and aware that the well-being of society and her own good are intimately tied to the good of the family, the church perceives in a more urgent and compelling way her mission of proclaiming to all people the plan of God for marriage and the family.[1]   — Pope John Paul II

I think the church does have a role in saying what's morally wrong. It's just that I disagree with their perception of what's morally wrong. In many ways I divorce God and Catholicism. I have to divorce what the church says from my relationship with God. I've learned that God is not anti-sexual and God doesn't judge us sexually in the same way the church does.   — Faye

I think to reconstruct the family it would take whole generations of reconstructing to make things better.

— Maya

The Catholic church is not my redeemer. Christ is. God is. The church is men. The church has nothing to do with my redemption, absolutely nothing. — Elizabeth

A nun once said to me, "To be healed you have to go back to the place where you were hurt." ... I also think that part of the reason that I'm in the church now, and probably the reason that most of us are, is because we're called to heal the church as much as the church is there to heal us.
— Faye

MY AIM IN conducting a feminist sociology from the standpoint of women was to make visible the fault lines between Catholic ideology and the realities it conceals. The life stories of eight women who grew up in Catholic homes suggest that Catholic family and sexual ideology helped to alienate them from the realities of their everyday/everynight lives, especially the realities they have come to name as incest. Out of their struggles to heal the points of rupture in their experiences of Catholic culture, they gained valuable insights about making gender and sexual relations more empowering for women and children.[2]

RELATIONSHIPS WITH THE CATHOLIC CHURCH: STORIES OF HEALING

For the past several years, the eight women who participated in my study have undergone a healing process, a process that has included challenging and countering the destructive aspects of Catholic family culture. As they healed they created a "new language"[3] for themselves, one based in part on acknowledging the *realities* of their everyday/everynight

Catholic family lives rather than accepting an *idealized* discourse about Catholic family life. For some of the women, staying within (or returning to) the Catholic church has brought healing. For others it hasn't. Yet all of the women are painfully aware of problems within the institutional church, and those who do remain in the church struggle to reconcile the often conflicting realities associated with healing from incest and being Catholic.

Cherrie, who has never left the church despite her criticism of the rigid and punitive Catholic culture of her childhood, has found her relationships with God, Jesus and the Blessed Mother to be invaluable sources of healing:

> I've had some very powerful experiences in my faith. In fact, I would say that in dealing with the incest, when it really all began to surface, it was actually God that I turned to first and he gave me the courage to go to people who would support me and help me get through it and deal with it.

Elizabeth returned to the Catholic church after a long stretch of having completely abandoned it. She emphasized that the real source of her spirituality does not come from her involvement in the "man-made" institutional church but from God and Jesus Christ:

> For about ten years myself I just completely abandoned the church and all its teachings. It was just, "I can't be bothered any more." And I think it was a period in my life that I had to grow and I had to do it another way. And the other way brought me back. Right now being Catholic is a source of strength and courage. It's not just being Catholic, it's being spiritual more than anything else ... The Catholic church is not my redeemer. Christ is. God is. The church is men. The church has nothing to do with my redemption, absolutely nothing.

Like Elizabeth, Faye eventually returned to the Catholic church after many years away from it. She found healing by "go[ing] back to the place where [she was] hurt." Transforming the image of an "anti-sexual" God was another vital part of healing:

> At first I had *no* desire to go back to the Catholic church
> — it never, never entered my mind. The idea was just ab-
> horrent to me. And then I got to the point where I was
> getting into an early forties crisis and my relationship with
> God was very important in my life but I'd hit a kind of a
> wall or a plateau and it wasn't going anywhere ... So I really
> prayed about what I should do next. I went to quite a
> number of Protestant churches but none of them seemed
> to be what I was looking for ... Then the first time I went
> to mass [after many years] I had the most incredible experi-
> ence. It was like that whole feeling of really being loved, it
> was like a feeling of coming home. The whole thing was so
> dramatic that I couldn't talk myself out of [becoming a
> Catholic again] ... A nun once said to me, "To be healed
> you have to go back to the place where you were hurt."
> And that always stuck in my mind ... So I've found the
> church healing in a number of different ways. I do find
> God in the church now and again, not all the time, just
> now and again, in things like sacraments and the mass and
> so on. Mostly I think I've found the church healing
> through the people who have helped me. A couple of
> priests I've found really, really helpful. About incest, too ...
> Today God is in many ways my best friend. It's a very un-
> conditional love. But when I was growing up God was the
> judge. It's just the opposite now. I'm past feeling that God
> would disapprove of me as a sexual person. I had to work
> at that because I can remember that initially I was afraid
> that God would disapprove of me sexually or disapprove of

sexual activity. God made sexual activity! But I grew up in a very anti-sexual culture and that was part of the Catholicism that I grew up in. It was very, very anti-sexual. And in many ways I divorce God and Catholicism ... I have to divorce what the church says from my relationship with God. I've learned that God is not anti-sexual, and God doesn't judge us sexually in the same way the church does.

It isn't surprising, then, that one of Faye's reasons for staying in the church is her belief that, especially in the area of sexuality, the church itself needs healing:

I also think that part of the reason that I'm in the church now, and probably the reason that most of us are, is because we're called to heal the church as much as the church is there to heal us. And as people who've been harmed by the church in many ways then we're the suppressed group you talk about in your research. We have more insight, so we can help heal the church in a way the hierarchy can't because they don't have the same perspective.

Mary's decision to stay in the church is similar:

I'm still in the struggle about being Catholic. I don't know what it is about [the Catholic] faith ... There was an angry stage I had and at that point it would have been tempting to just leave ... But I don't feel I can criticize [the church] unless I remain a part of it. Especially the things I don't like, like the ordination of women. I feel it's despicable that it hasn't changed yet. It's just a man-made rule. And so I feel I can really be vocal about it from the inside, not the outside looking in.

By remaining with the church, Mary has been able to transform in creative ways some negative aspects of her Catholic childhood. Mary's encounter with a priest is especially powerful when we recall her agonizing experiences with the sacraments of confession and Holy Communion:

> When I did this soul-searching about the church one thing that came up through counselling was the problem with the whole act of forgiveness. It was no good for my [non-Catholic] counsellor to say to me, "You're forgiven." It just wasn't working — it didn't assure me. So I went to a priest [who was a special friend] and explained that I needed to go through the actual ritual of confession because somewhere it was stuck in there that I wasn't truly forgiven. I just knew that I went to Communion over and over again with sin on my soul. So he asked me to help him walk through it with him because he didn't know the steps. He asked me to be his guide. He asked permission for everything and at each step he asked me, "Do I have to do this?" And I said, "Yes! I want the works. This is how I see this, almost as an exorcism. You're getting rid of everything negative that's still in there." So he went through it [the ritual of confession] just as if I were a young child and it was beautiful. And the tears that I did expel were totally of joyful freedom, there was no sorrow. It was wonderful, it wasn't a morbid, depressing experience, it was wonderful — almost like the sun was coming in ... I think I would have been tortured all my days with whatever baggage I had if I hadn't had this wonderful experience of being bathed and feeling whole. Maybe I do have a stronger faith than I want to admit, in grace ... I feel like I've been free of the trappings of the church ever since. After that I could stand back and really see politics for what it is, and the structure, see them as separate from the people that I know within [the church] who are doing good things. I don't confuse the two any more. So it was a very healthy

experience. I feel like before I was just sort of crawling through life and now I feel like I have been birthed. I've gone through the ritual.

Maya, the only participant born in the era of Vatican II Catholicism who still formally defines herself as a Catholic, emphasized that she's careful to abide by only those church teachings that promote her healing. For her the Christian motto, "Love your neighbour as yourself," is one that helps her to heal relationships with family members, friends and with herself. But she rejects many Catholic tenets, such as those opposing divorce, the entrance of women into the priesthood and premarital sex. At the same time, she still finds it difficult to challenge her family's strong beliefs about sexuality:

> These days I'm much more up front and more assertive and that's partly to do with giving words to things and saying how I feel — even though it may still be taboo and hard to do. I'm much more courageous. Though I can't say that I've been courageous enough to deal with the issue of sexuality. I've had to take smaller steps than that. Sexuality still feels really big.

Although Courage no longer attends mass, her "faith in a spiritual being" has been a crucial part of her healing. For Courage, having faith doesn't mean she has to formally participate in church rituals and sacraments:

> [A priest who passed away recently] helped me come to my understanding of God. He explained that I don't have to go to church to have a relationship with God. At first I was threatened by him being in the church ... I think if he were still alive he'd be one of the people trying to make changes in the church. Another guy, a priest, he's hardly

like a priest, I had my confession done in his car, which was okay by me. Both of those priests said you don't have to go to church to be forgiven and to have an understanding of who God is.

These days Content tends to be indifferent toward the Catholic church — the church hasn't been part of her healing:

I've had no healing from the church. It's partly because I'm not really a religious person. I believe the church helps some people spiritually but it's not for me, at least not yet. Maybe some time in the future, like when I have children, but not for now ... People ask me all the time why I don't go to church and I think, "Why should I go to church to prove that I believe in God?" I don't want the church to control me. I'd like to know where all those rules came from, like having to go to church every week and having to go to confession before you can take Communion ... To me God's love is more unconditional than that.

In a similar way, Jackie simply chooses not to belong to a church that, in her experience, doesn't value women:

Even as a child I think I was aware that women weren't really valued [in the Catholic church]. Because when you went to church and you sat there and heard about this man, this Father-God, and Jesus, there was never any mention about women. And when there was, it was the women who were washing his feet or whatever, women who didn't really play an important role ... I don't spend as much time thinking about the church any more and sort of blaming that whole ideology of father as the ruler. I just move on with my life and say, "Well, that's not part of my life. I'm not going to worry about that any more. I can't change the church so, at the same time, I don't have to be part of it."

Redefining Gender and Sexual Relations: Challenging Catholic Family and Sexual Ideology

In recent decades, feminists have been engaged in the enormous tasks of resisting male dominance, trying to improve women's socio-economic status and challenging the conflation of womanhood with sexuality, fertility and work in the home.[4] They have lobbied for structural changes — such as full-time, well-paying work for women, and state-funded day care programs[5] — that allow for the emergence of alternatives to a patriarchal family model.[6]

In responding to incest as a specific form of abuse, feminists are aware that we are facing a complex set of structural and cultural influences — including religious ideologies that promote patriarchy as something "natural" and "divinely ordained." Some feminists have focused their energy on patriarchal religious institutions such as the Catholic church by pushing for structural changes that will bring about deep and lasting change in the realm of gender and sexual relations. In western societies, the demand for change from feminists has been strengthened both by overall improvements in women's socio-economic status and by the shift toward secularism. Yet the question remains: Has this been enough?

According to the participants in my study, Catholicism still has a long way to go. These women don't have all the answers, but they did offer some ways of challenging Catholic family and sexual ideology. They agreed that we need to "do away" with traditional family relations. Elizabeth reminded us that gender roles need to be redefined for both men and women if we are going to have families that promote mutuality:

> The church is also imposing on men. It's imposing on men
> a system that says, "You have to be the powerful one. You
> have to be the boss. You have to demand respect." That's

not mutuality. They're teaching [men] power. Abusive power. So the church is not playing with a full deck when it comes to men. We keep saying, "Poor women, poor women." But men have these dominant roles and half of them don't want them, they don't know what to do with them: "head of the household," "the strong one." They're not even allowed to grieve and weep. A lot of men still don't know how to do that. So [the church] isn't giving them a chance to be mutual in partnership and in relationship. They're still saying, "You have to be the dominant one." And that's where the church goes wrong. And that's where we go wrong when we say, "It's just the women who are suffering in the church." It's easy to focus on that because we've suffered longer.

In the realm of Catholic mothering, Faye expressed frustration over Pope John Paul II's insistence that women's place is still, in the final analysis, in the home. At the same time, she expressed concern about devaluing the traditional work of women and suggested that a redistribution of economic resources would allow women to be paid a living wage to perform those necessary tasks:

> I think the Pope is fighting a losing battle when it comes to keeping women in their "natural" place. I have very mixed feelings about that because I think women who want to be mothers and want to raise kids should feel that this is a really valid kind of choice. But again, I think it should be a choice. I wouldn't want to see that elevated as the only role for women. But I'd certainly like to see it elevated as a more important role for women. A lot of women who really want to stay home just feel dismissed by society. Many women talk about how devalued they feel because they're not out working and they don't have a

profession. And that's wrong, too. I think it's a very valuable role. And some women are very good at it. If our society was different and we actually paid women to stay home for being mothers then it would be a real, valid choice for them and they could choose to leave then and still get paid for what they're doing. That's what I'd like to see. But we'd have to restructure our whole social network. If we really valued children that's what we would do — but we don't value children enough.

As for sexuality and the Catholic church, these women aren't very optimistic. Mary doesn't believe that changes since Vatican II have made much of a difference when it comes to recognizing that "sex isn't a dirty word":

> It's still all lumped together like a bad act, except under certain conditions, mostly to have children ... [We've learned that Catholicism] is like algebra, like mathematics. We have these two things and if they don't equal that then they're wrong. That's it. There's no way around it. I hate that about the church and I don't think it has anything to do with faith. It's the rules we're making into our religion. It's like, where's the faith part of it?

Having reflected on her struggle to overcome the deep sense of unworthiness she felt in the realm of sexuality, Elizabeth believes that "the majority of the church's teachings still need to be examined." Faye said that even though the church is more open today to discussing sexuality, there should be more emphasis on identifying abusive sex in families. She suggested returning to a Catholic notion of sin but one that would only recognize *abusive* sex — not healthy, mutual sexual relationships — as sinful. Faye gave the example of her own sexually abusive marriage to show that an institutionally sanctioned relationship is no guarantee of mutuality:

I think [the church hierarchy] has a basic conflict between supporting the family, seeing all the terrible things that can happen to people in families, and really speaking out about this kind of stuff — not just sexual abuse but also alcoholism and violence. I think the church is changing somewhat in the sense that they'll actually talk about things like sexual abuse but they don't talk about it enough. The church has been forced to deal with sexual abuse because of the sexual abuse by clergy ... God knows how many times I sit in mass and think, "I know statistically that there are all kinds of kids sitting here at mass who are being abused." But they never come out and say, "It's always wrong to have sex with children. It's always wrong." I don't know why they never say that. It sounds so trivial in some ways that the church should say this so openly and often but what strikes me is that they never say it. It's the one place they should be saying it! They're so concerned with supporting "the family," wanting the family to stay strong. If they changed the emphasis on keeping families together and keeping families strong, if they emphasized more the dignity and integrity of the person and children as being more important than any kind of image of the family it would be a whole lot better ... [The clergy in the church] hardly ever talk about sin any more. I think there *is* such a thing as sexual sin. It's abusive sex, where you're using another person for your own needs without any regard for them as a person. That's sexual sin. It's certainly my understanding of it now and I think it's God's understanding of it, too ... It's not the type of relationship that's important, it's the attitude ... I wish the church would recognize that even a monogamous marriage can be abusive. I mean, certainly when I look back on my own marriage it was sexually abusive. And that, according to the church, was the only relationship in which sex was okay.

∾

Breaking silence about any kind of oppression is a difficult
political act. Given the taboos against challenging Catholic
family and sexual ideology, breaking silence about incest in
Catholic families may be nothing short of revolutionary. The
lives of these eight women attest to the fact that transforming
gender and sexual relations requires courageous, revolutionary patience.[7] Their lives also attest to the fact that taking a
stand against Catholic family and sexual ideology is not necessarily a simple act of rejecting the Catholic church. Rather,
it may be a matter of demanding that the church rethink gender and sexuality in light of its commitment to social justice.
If we believe that we can change the Catholic church, and
that it is worth our while to do so, we might look to people
like Faye, a woman who has been harmed by the church yet
whose continuing presence within it is facilitating healing
and change.

As we clarify the difference between religious ideology
(the use of religion to sanction and maintain unjust social relations) and theology (the use of religion to promote just and
mutual human relationships) some difficult questions
emerge: What should we preserve from Catholic teachings?
And to what extent can justice-minded Catholics take ownership of the faith even while the "powers that be" remain entrenched in a patriarchal and authoritarian mindset?

When I began this study, I believed that the standpoint of
incest survivors who grew up in Catholic homes would provide a sound critique of Catholic family culture. Their standpoint has provided just such a critique. Of course, incestuous
sexual abuse is far from being a phenomenon found exclu-
sively within Catholic families. But what became clear
through the case studies of eight Catholic families is that

there were definite fault lines for these women within Catholic family culture. Incest thrived in a culture that endorsed male power and privilege. It thrived in a culture in which girls and women (especially mothers) found it difficult, and often impossible, to challenge male power in their homes. And it thrived in a culture marked by secrecy, shame and punishment in the realm of sexuality.

This book is about politicizing "the Catholic family." In writing it, I was guided by other second-wave feminists who succeeded in politicizing gender and sexual relations within the "private" sphere. This book is also about social justice, especially the call for us to move beyond an analysis of individual acts of injustice toward an analysis of unjust structures and practices.[8] Finally, in its attempt to show that feminist praxis contributes in vital ways to social justice, this book is about *sexual* justice — one of the most trivialized, feared and postponed dimensions of social justice in the world today.[9] Clearly, if the Catholic church were to begin taking seriously a feminist analysis of gender and sexuality, there would be deep and radical consequences for Catholic teachings on family life and sexuality. The task now seems to be to continue resisting, struggling and grappling with the questions, especially how a "marriage" of feminism and Catholicism's principles of social justice might guide our efforts to reconstruct gender and sexual relations within families and society as a whole.

Appendix I

Summary of Research Objectives

My name is Tish Langlois and I'm doing a research project to fulfil requirements for a Master of Women's Studies degree at Memorial University of Newfoundland. I am conducting a qualitative study with women incest survivors who grew up in Catholic homes.

Two counsellors in town agreed to help me identify potential participants. I invite you to read this summary and consider joining my study. During the course of the study I will conduct two sets of individual and group interviews.

Ethical considerations in conducting research with incest survivors require that I take a number of measures to protect the participants:

i) Only women who are active in a survivors' group and/or individual counselling will be invited to participate.

ii) Pseudonyms will be used to conceal the identity of participants and the identity of family members and friends named during the interviews.

iii) The researcher, the participants and any research assistants will be required to sign an oath of confidentiality.

iv) Each participant will be required to sign a consent form *a)* at the commencement of the study and *b)* at the completion of the study.

v) Participants will be free to withdraw from the study at any time.

vi) Cassettes and transcripts will be stored in a locked file box.

vii) Participants should be aware that the findings of this study may be published in popular/scholarly journals or in book form.

If you would like to find out more about the study, please inform your counsellor or contact me directly. Thank you!

— Tish Langlois

Appendix II

Individual Interview Guide #1

INTRODUCTION:

The purpose of this research is to explore possible connections between incest and Catholic family culture. This is the first of two in-depth interviews. The questions are open-ended. If you wish to skip a question or come back to it later in the interview, please feel free to do so.

INCEST:

1. With as much detail as you feel comfortable, please describe the circumstances surrounding your history of incest. Who were the main actors? When did it occur? Please give as many details as possible which will help to describe the atmosphere and circumstances of your family life before, during and after the incest.

2. From your own experience, reading and reflection, why do you think incest happens?

CATHOLIC FAMILY CULTURE:

1. Reflecting on your own experience, in what ways was/is your family a "Catholic" family?

2. In what ways might there have been connections between your family's Catholic values and the incest?

3. Were/are there some benefits to your family's commitment to Catholicism? Did Catholicism help you in any way to deal with the incest?

APPENDIX III

INDIVIDUAL INTERVIEW GUIDE #2

QUESTIONS:

1. If at all, how has your participation in the study to date contributed to your understanding of the connections between incest and Catholic family culture?

2. Please describe any possible connections between Catholicism and women's (e.g., a mother's, a daughter's) powerlessness. Reflecting on your family experience, in what ways might your mother's position have affected her ability to protect you?

3. If you could go back in time and change some things about your family's history what changes would you make?

4. If you were given the opportunity to reconstruct family relations in general, what recommendations would you make?

5. What role, if any, would you see the Catholic church playing in these reconstructed relations?

APPENDIX IV

FOCUS GROUP INTERVIEW GUIDE #1

INTRODUCTION:

The purpose of a focus group discussion is to encourage participants to explore the subject in depth and to provide a forum for participants to learn from one another. Please feel free to speak as you wish, bearing in mind that the goal of the discussion is to get input from all participants. The researcher will act as the facilitator. A qualified counsellor, chosen and approved by the research participants, will join the focus group discussion. The counsellor will be available in the event that a participant feels uncomfortable and needs time, within the group or in private, to talk.

INCEST AND CATHOLIC FAMILY CULTURE:

1. With as much detail as you feel comfortable, please introduce yourself to the group and describe the circumstances surrounding your history of incest.

2. Do you think there are important differences between incest and sexual abuse committed by a non-family member? If so, please elaborate.

3. Given your own experience and reflection since the first individual interview, do you think there are connections between your family's Catholic values and your history of incest? What might these be?

4. How may Catholicism's insistence on patriarchal authority (both within the family and the institutional church) have played a role in the incest?

5. What role do you see your mother having played in your history of incest? Do you see any ways in which Catholicism's emphasis on women's primary roles as mothers and wives may have connected to your incest history?

6. How are you feeling about the focus group discussion?

APPENDIX V

FOCUS GROUP INTERVIEW GUIDE #2

Researcher's note: I introduced this focus group discussion by handing out a copy of "An abuse of journalistic privilege: Local commentator takes action over CBC-Radio broadcast" to each participant. The article was a response to a paper and radio interview I gave in December of 1994.

QUESTIONS:

1. What is your response to this article?

2. How are you feeling about your participation in the research process to date?

3. Do you have any feedback on the preliminary [October 1994] or secondary [March 1995] reports?

4. Please explore, from your own experience, any differences between the pre and post Vatican II period in Catholic families.

5. Please explore, again from your own experience, the role of your mother in your incest history.

6. What additional thoughts do you have on the possible connection between incest and Catholic family culture?

7. How are you feeling about this focus group discussion?

APPENDIX VI

CONSENT FORM FOR PARTICIPANTS AND COUNSELLORS

The purpose of this study is to explore possible connections between incest and Catholic family culture.

Potential participants are invited to join a study which may help to end the cycle of sexual violence in families, Catholic families in particular. The results of this study may be made available to relevant groups and publishers who have an interest in ending family violence. Individual participants may benefit from joining with other survivors of incest to explore the causes of sexual violence against women.

The study will take place over a one-year period. It will consist of at least two extensive individual interviews and two focus group discussions about incest in Catholic families.

I understand that all interview transcripts will be stored in a locked file cabinet. I understand that participants' names will not appear on transcripts; pseudonyms will be used. I understand that the risks to the participants are twofold. First, participants may find the subject matter disturbing. Therefore, only participants who are presently involved in a group for survivors of sexual abuse and/or are receiving counselling related to their history of incest will be invited to participate. Second, while every effort will be made to ensure confidentiality and to protect the anonymity of participants (for instance, through the use of pseudonyms) being identified as a participant in this study is a possibility. Participants need to be aware of this potential risk. The limitations on confidentiality are threefold: a) information surfacing about the abuse of a current minor, b) threats of harm against another person, and c) stopping an act of suicide.

As the research proceeds, transcripts and interpretations of the data will be made available to the participants. A second consent form will be presented to the participants (to release the data for publication) at the completion of the study.

I understand that I am free to withdraw from the study at any time without prejudice. In other words, participants may withdraw their written consent after it has been granted to the researcher.

I _____ (research participant) understand the terms of this study, agree to abide by these conditions and consent to participate.

Signed _____ (research participant)

Date _____

Researcher (Tish Langlois) _____

Date _____

Referring Counsellor _____

Date _____

Appendix VII

Oath of Confidentiality

To be signed by all people involved in the study, including: the researcher, research participants, research assistants and counsellors.

I _____ understand that information shared during the research process, including the actual names of participants, shall be kept in confidence. I agree not to reveal information about the study beyond those who are involved in the study (that is, those who have also signed an oath of confidentiality).

Signed _____

Date _____

Researcher _____

Date _____

APPENDIX VIII

CONSENT TO HAVE INTERVIEWS AUDIOTAPED

I _____ consent to have the interviews audiotaped. I understand that tapes will be erased following submission and acceptance of the thesis. I understand that, in the case that a research assistant is hired to transcribe the interviews, the research assistant will be required to sign an oath of confidentiality. I understand that tapes and transcripts will be stored in a locked file cabinet. I understand that pseudonyms will be used to identify participants.

Signed _____

Date _____

Principal Researcher _____

Date _____

APPENDIX IX

CONSENT FORM TO RELEASE RESEARCH DATA

I have participated in a study conducted by Tish Langlois. I have read the interpretations of the data and been given an opportunity to comment on these interpretations.

I _____ consent to release the data and interpretations of the data for publication in the thesis. I am aware that the results of this study may be published in popular/scholarly journals or in book form.

I am aware that audiotapes of recorded interviews will be erased upon submission of the thesis. I am aware that the master list, which matches actual names to pseudonyms, will be destroyed upon submission of the thesis. I understand that transcripts will not list actual names of participants but will be identified through the use of pseudonyms. I am aware that the researcher wishes to hold on to interview transcripts for three years after the date of thesis submission, during which time the transcripts will be stored in a locked file cabinet and after which time the transcripts will be destroyed. The transcripts may be needed to prepare results of the study for future publication.

Signed _____

Date _____

Principal Researcher _____

Date _____

NOTES

INTRODUCTION

1. Carter Heyward, *Touching Our Strength: The Erotic as Power and the Love of God* (San Francisco: Harper and Row, 1989), 4.

2. In the late 1980s several Catholic priests in the Archdiocese of St. John's, Newfoundland, were convicted of sexual assault and gross indecency committed against pubescent altar boys. Concurrent with the public disclosures involving priests in the Archdiocese, disclosures of sexual and physical abuse from the 1970s at the Mount Cashel Orphanage began to surface. The orphanage was run by the Congregation of Christian Brothers. Public concern led to the appointment of a Royal Commission of Inquiry headed by retired Justice Samuel Hughes.

3. Working Group on Child Sexual Abuse, *Brief Submission to the Special Commission of Enquiry into Sexual Abuse of Children by members of the Clergy* (St. John's, NF: Working Group on Child Sexual Abuse, 1989), 1.

4. Canadian Conference of Catholic Bishops, *From Pain to Hope: Report from the CCCB Ad Hoc Committee on Child Sexual Abuse* (Ottawa: CCCB, 1992), 41.

5. *The Report of the Archdiocesan Commission of Enquiry in the Sexual Abuse of Children by Members of the Clergy* (St. John's, NF: Archdiocese of St. John's, 1990). The report, commonly known as the Winter Commission, was released in June of 1990. The commission was established by the Archbishop of St. John's and, although not officially established under the *Public Enquiries Act,* used a process modelled on that of a public enquiry. The enquiry was limited to the sexual abuse of male children.

6. My use of the term "incest" refers to "incestuous sexual abuse" and is not intended to refer to sexual activity between mutually consenting relatives, as, for instance, in the case of marriage between first cousins. For simplicity's sake I use "incest" rather than "incestuous sexual abuse" throughout the book.

7. Scholars in North America and abroad have begun a strong feminist critique of the Judeo-Christian tradition. See, for example, Mary Daly, *Beyond God the Father* (Boston: Beacon Press, 1973); Mary Daly, "After the Death of God the Father," in Carol P. Christ and Judith Plascow, eds., *Womanspirit Rising: A Feminist Reader in Religion* (San Francisco: HarperCollins, 1979), 53-62; Rosemary Radford Ruether, "The Western Religious Tradition and Violence Against Women in the Home," in Joanne Carlson Brown and Carole R. Bohn, eds., *Christianity, Patriarchy and Abuse* (New York: Pilgrim Press, 1989), 31–41; Florence Rush, *The Best Kept Secret: Sexual Abuse of Children* (Englewood Cliffs, NJ: Prentice-Hall, 1980); and Eileen Zieget Silberman, *The Savage Sacrament: A Theology of Marriage After American Feminism* (Mystic, CT: Twenty-Third Publications, 1983). See also more recent publications, including Carol J. Adams and Marie M. Fortune, *Violence Against Women and Children: A Christian Theological Sourcebook* (New York: Continuum Publishing Company, 1995); and Anne Bathurst Gilson, *Eros Breaking Free: Interpreting Sexual Theo-Ethics* (Cleveland: The Pilgrim Press, 1995).

8. See Daly, *Beyond God the Father* and "After the Death of God the Father"; and Radford Ruether, "The Western Religious Tradition and Violence Against Women in the Home."

9. Heyward, *Touching Our Strength.*

10. See Daly, *Beyond God the Father;* Radford Ruether, "The Western Religious Tradition and Violence Against Women in the Home"; Uta Ranke-Heinemann, *Eunuchs for Heaven: The Catholic Church and Sexuality* (London: Andre Deutsch, 1990); and Sheila A. Redmond, "Christian 'Virtues' and Recovery From Child Sexual Abuse," in Brown and Bohn, eds., *Christianity, Patriarchy and Abuse*, 70–88.

11. See Carole R. Bohn, "Dominion to Rule: The Roots and Consequences of a Theology of Ownership," in Brown and Bohn, eds., *Christianity, Patriarchy and Abuse*, 105–116; and Rush, *The Best Kept Secret.*

12. Canadian Conference of Catholic Bishops, *From Pain to Hope.*

13. See Redmond, "Christian 'Virtues' and Recovery From Child Sexual Abuse."

14. Daly, *Beyond God the Father.*

15. Rush, *The Best Kept Secret*; Annie Imbens and Inneke Jonker, *Christianity and Incest* (Minneapolis: Fortress Press, 1992); Carolyn Holderread Heggen, *Sexual Abuse in Christian Homes and Churches* (Scottdale, PA: Herald Press, 1993).

16. "An Abuse of Journalistic Privilege: Local Commentator Takes Action Over CBC-Radio Broadcast," *The Monitor: Newfoundland's Catholic Journal* (February 1995), 2.

17. Sandra Harding explores the notion of "the right time in history" in her article, "Starting Thought From Women's Lives: Eight Points for Maximizing Objectivity," *Journal of Social Philosophy* 21, nos. 2/3 (1991), 141–149.

18. See Michael T. Ryan, *Solidarity: Christian Social Teaching and Canadian Society* (London, ON: Guided Study Programs in the Catholic Faith, 1990).

19. Paulo Freire, *Pedagogy of the Oppressed* (New York: Herder and Herder, 1971).

20. I am indebted to Carter Heyward for my use of the term "erotophobia," especially as it appears in *Touching Our Strength: The Erotic as Power and the Love of God.*

21. Heyward, *Touching Our Strength,* 4.

22. See especially Kate Millett's "Sexual Politics: A Manifesto for Revolution," in Anne Koedt, Ellen Levine and Anita Rapone, eds., *Radical Feminism* (New York: Quadrangle Books, 1973), 365–367.

23. I place quotation marks around "the family" for two reasons. First, it highlights the use of the term in official Catholic writings. Second, it is intended to indicate a critique of the assumption that there is, or ought to be, a single family structure. According to Canadian sociologist Margrit Eichler, "the *monolithic bias* expresses itself in a tendency to treat the family as a monolithic structure, and in an emphasis on uniformity of experience and universality of structure and functions rather than on diversity of experiences, structures and functions. The *conservative bias* expresses itself in the tendency to either largely ignore recent changes [in family structure], or to treat them as ephemeral, rather than comprehending them as central and fundamental," *Families in Canada Today: Recent Changes and Their Policy Implications* (Toronto: Gage Educational Publishing Company, 1988), 2.

24. This is not the first time in history that there have been attempts to build bridges between Christian social teaching and secular movements for social change. A movement called Christian socialism, for example, seeking to "Christianize Marxism," arose in the late nineteenth century. See Ryan, *Solidarity,* 9.

25. See especially Sandra Harding, "Rethinking Standpoint Epistemology: What is 'Strong Objectivity'?," in Elizabeth Potter and Linda

Alcoff, eds., *Feminist Epistemologies* (New York: Routledge, Chapman and Hall, 1993), 49–82; Harding, "Starting Thought from Women's Lives"; Dorothy Smith, *The Conceptual Practices of Power* (Toronto: University of Toronto Press, 1990) and *The Everyday World as Problematic* (Boston: Northeastern University Press, 1987).

26. Smith explores the concept of lines of fault especially in part two of *The Everyday World as Problematic.*

27. I gratefully acknowledge the financial assistance I received from Memorial University of Newfoundland's Institute of Social and Economic Research (ISER) which supported three trips to the research site.

28. Leonard Desroches, *Allow the Water: Anger, Fear, Power, Work, Sexuality, Community — and the Spirituality and Practice of Non-Violence* (Toronto: Dunamis Publishers, 1996).

CHAPTER I

1. For a good introduction to feminist standpoint theory see Sandra Harding, "Starting Thought from Women's Lives: Eight Points for Maximizing Objectivity," *Journal of Social Philosophy* 21, nos. 2/3 (1991), 141-149. For a discussion of feminist sociology from the standpoint of women see Dorothy E. Smith, *The Everyday World as Problematic* (Boston: Northeastern University Press, 1987).

2. My research design was influenced by a tradition of action and empowerment-oriented feminist research. For a synopsis of this tradition see Shulamit Reinharz, *Feminist Methods in Social Research* (New York: Oxford University Press, 1992), 181-186. See also Patricia Maguire, *Doing Participatory Research: A Feminist Approach* (Amherst, MA: Centre for International Education, 1987); and Janice L. Ristock and Joan Pennell, *Community Research as Empowerment: Feminist Links, Postmodern Interruptions* (Toronto: Oxford University Press, 1996).

3. For more about sexual justice see especially Carter Heyward, *Touching Our Strength: The Erotic as Power and the Love of God* (San Francisco: Harper and Row, 1989). An excellent sourcebook on the evolution of sexual justice among Christian feminists is Carol J. Adams and Marie M. Fortune, eds., *Violence Against Women and Children: A Christian Theological Sourcebook* (New York: Continuum Publishing Company, 1995).

4. *Ethical Guidelines* (St. John's, NF: Memorial University of Newfoundland, School of Social Work, Human Subjects Research Committee, 1993).

5. I took the following additional measures to protect the participants. Prior to signing the consent form (Appendix VI) participants were made aware of the possibility that the study would be published. The participants' anonymity (beyond the research group) was respected throughout. Before the interviews began, the participants signed the consent form and the oath of confidentiality (Appendix VII). This helped participants to feel free to speak openly during the focus group discussions. The oath of confidentiality also reinforced that the anonymity of the other research participants was to be protected. The participants also signed a form giving consent to have the interviews taped (Appendix VIII). At the close of the study, each participant signed a consent form to release the information given during the interviews (Appendix IX).

6. Patricia Maguire, *Doing Participatory Research: A Feminist Approach* (MA: Centre for International Education, 1987), 10.

7. Maguire, *Doing Participatory Research*, 9-10. See also William Foot Whyte, ed., *Participatory Action Research* (Newbury Park, CA: Sage Publications, 1991).

8. Sandra Kirby and Kate McKenna, *Experience, Research, Social Change: Methods from the Margins* (Toronto: Garamond Press, 1989).

9. Ibid., 170.

10. For a guide to qualitative research see, for example, Catherine Marshall and Gretchen B. Rossman, *Designing Qualitative Research* (Newbury Park, CA: Sage Publications, 1989).

11. Robert K. Yin, *Case Study Research: Design and Methods* (Thousand Oaks, CA: Sage Publications, 1994), 30-31.

12. For my use of the term "everyday/everynight lives" I am indebted to Dorothy Smith.

13. Maguire, *Doing Participatory Research*.

14. The first set of interviews was based on notes rather than audiotapes. Therefore about 20 per cent of interview excerpts that appear in later chapters are based on notes rather than transcriptions. The interview notes were approved by the interviewees — in three cases slight amendments were made before approval was granted. Throughout the research process participants were sent reports on the interviews. A preliminary

report was sent in October of 1994, after the first set of individual interviews and the first focus group interview (held in August of 1994). I sent a secondary report in March of 1995, after the second set of individual interviews (held in December of 1994). The final focus group discussion was held at the end of March of 1995, after participants had a chance to read the secondary report. As I prepared the book manuscript I conducted one final set of individual interviews. The reports to participants served several purposes. They allowed me to a) prepare the participants for future visits to the research site, b) provide for the participants a sampling of excerpts, c) summarize the emergent themes from the interviews, and d) give my preliminary analysis of the interviews. I encouraged the participants to express their agreement or disagreement with my analysis and I promised to present, in the text of my thesis/book, any points of difference between my views and theirs.

15. See, for example, Reinharz, *Feminist Methods in Social Research*, 33.

16. For a discussion of focus groups as a qualitative method see David L. Morgan, *Focus Groups as Qualitative Research* (Newbury Park, CA: Sage Publications, 1988).

17. At the suggestion of my supervisors, I asked a qualified counsellor to be present during both focus group discussions in the event that someone needed a break or felt uncomfortable.

18. Pope John Paul II, On the Family: Familiaris Consortio (Rome: Vatican Council, 1981), 23; Pope Leo XIII, Arcanum Divinae Sapientae, in Odile M. Liebard, ed., *Official Catholic Teachings: Love and Sexuality* (1880; reprinted, Wilmington, NC: McGrath Publishing Company, 1978); Pope Pius XI, Casti Connubii, in Odile M. Liebard, ed., *Official Catholic Teachings: Love and Sexuality* (1930; reprinted, Wilmington, NC: McGrath Publishing Company, 1978); and the Reverend George A. Kelly, *The Catholic Marriage Manual* (New York: Random House, 1958).

CHAPTER 2

1. It is beyond the scope of this book to detail the variety of feminisms. For an introduction to theories of feminism see Alison M. Jaggar, *Feminist Politics and Human Nature* (Totowa, NJ: Rowman and Littlefield Publishers, 1988).

2. Jaggar, *Feminist Politics and Human Nature*, 123.

3. I am aware of postmodern critiques of feminist standpoint theory that highlight the latter's tendency to gloss over differences in women's experiences and to assume that there is a single dominant group and a single social world. See, for example, Janice L. Ristock and Joan Pennell, *Community Research as Empowerment: Feminist Links, Postmodern Interruptions* (Toronto: Oxford University Press, 1996), 5-6.

4. See, for example, the collection of essays by scholars who have adopted Smith's approach to social analysis: Marie Campbell and Ann Manicom, eds., *Knowledge, Experience, and Ruling Relations: Studies in the Social Organization of Knowledge* (Toronto: University of Toronto Press, 1995).

5. Alison M. Jaggar, "Political Philosophies of Women's Liberation," in Laurel Richardson and Verta Taylor, eds., *Feminist Frontiers: Rethinking Sex, Gender and Society* (Reading, MA: Addison-Wesley Publishing Company, 1983), 322.

6. One of the earliest critiques of the nuclear family in the Marxist tradition is in Friedrich Engels's, *The Origin of the Family, Private Property and the State* (1942; reprint New York: International Publishers, 1972).

7. Jaggar, "Political Philosophies of Women's Liberation," 324.

8. Ibid., 325.

9. For an example of early radical feminist theorizing see Radicalesbians's, "The Woman Identified Woman," in Anne Koedt, Ellen Levine and Anita Rapone, eds., *Radical Feminism* (New York: Quadrangle Books, 1973), 240-245.

10. During my 1989-1990 academic year at the University of Toronto I first read Adrienne Rich's "Compulsory Heterosexuality and Lesbian Existence," *Signs* 5 (1980), 631-660. I was simultaneously shocked and delighted by her insights. Her critique played a central role in the formation of my critique of Catholic teachings on marriage and the family.

11. Rich, "Compulsory Heterosexuality and Lesbian Existence," 647-648.

12. Jaggar, *Feminist Politics and Human Nature*, 124.

13. Ibid., 132.

14. There is debate about the use of the term "gendered (or gender) division of labour" versus "sexual division of labour." Some feminists, Alison M. Jaggar and Nancy Hartsock, for example, prefer the term "sexual division of labour" because of their belief that "the division of labour

between women and men is not yet entirely a social affair (women and not men still bear children)," Alison M. Jaggar, *Feminist Politics and Human Nature*, 163. My use of the term "gendered division of labour" has been influenced by Canadian sociologist Meg Luxton. See "Two Hands for the Clock: Changing Patterns in the Gendered Division of Labour in the Home," in Meg Luxton, Harriet Rosenberg and Sedef Arat Koc, eds., *Through the Kitchen Window: The Politics of Home and Family* (Toronto: Garamond Press, 1990), 39-55. For some background on this debate see, for example, Susan J. Kessler and Wendy McKenna, *Gender: An Ethnomethodological Approach* (Chicago: University of Chicago Press, 1978).

15. Nancy Hartsock, "The Feminist Standpoint: Developing the Ground for a Specifically Feminist Historical Materialism," in Sandra Harding and Merrill B. Hintikka, eds., *Discovering Reality* (London: D. Reidel Publishing Company, 1983), 284.

16. Ibid., 304.

17. For a detailed explanation of feminist standpoint theory see Sandra Harding, "Starting Thought from Women's Lives: Eight Points for Maximizing Objectivity," *Journal of Social Philosophy* 21, nos. 2/3 (1991); and Sandra Harding, "Rethinking Standpoint Epistemology: What Is 'Strong Objectivity'?," in Elizabeth Potter and Linda Alcoff, eds., *Feminist Epistemologies* (New York: Routledge, Chapman and Hall, 1993), 49-82. For a more in-depth analysis see Sandra Harding, *The Science Question in Feminism* (Ithaca: Cornell University Press, 1986); and Sandra Harding, *Whose Science? Whose Knowledge? Thinking From Women's Lives* (Ithaca: Cornell University Press, 1991).

18. Harding, "Starting Thought from Women's Lives," 140.

19. Brazilian educator Paulo Freire developed this extensively in *Pedagogy of the Oppressed* (New York: Herder and Herder, 1971).

20. Harding, "Starting Thought from Women's Lives," 144.

21. Harding defends Hartsock's use of the term "real relations" in the following way: "Hartsock's use of the term 'real relations' may suggest to some readers that she and other standpoint theorists are hopelessly mired in an epistemology and metaphysics that have been discredited by social constructionists. The judgment fails to appreciate the way standpoint theories reject *both* pure realist and pure social constructionist epistemologies and metaphysics." Harding, "Rethinking Standpoint Epistemology," 77-78.

22. Harding, "Starting Thought from Women's Lives," 144.

23. Harding, "Rethinking Standpoint Epistemology," 61.

24. Harding, "Starting Thought from Women's Lives," 144.

25. Smith, *The Conceptual Practices of Power*, 206.

26. James Louis Heap, "Forward" to Campbell and Manicom, eds., *Knowledge, Experience and Ruling Relations*, ix-x.

27. Smith, *The Conceptual Practices of Power*, 14.

28. Dorothy E. Smith, "Women, Class and Family," in *Women, Class, Family and the State* (Toronto: Garamond Books, 1985), 2.

29. Dorothy E. Smith, *The Everyday World as Problematic* (Boston: Northeastern University Press, 1987), 55.

30. Ibid., 54.

31. Ibid.

32. Smith, *The Conceptual Practices of Power*, 13.

33. Ibid., 19.

34. Smith, *The Everyday World as Problematic*.

35. Gillian Walker, *Family Violence and the Women's Movement: The Conceptual Politics of Struggle* (Toronto: University of Toronto Press, 1990), 8.

36. Ibid., 9.

37. In this study it is important to recognize that, while Catholic ideology in its textual form has changed very little over time, practices within Catholic families have changed a great deal, especially since Vatican II and second-wave feminism. The relevance to this study of the decline in the efficacy of Catholicism within Canadian society since the 1960s is discussed in Chapter 5.

38. Carter Heyward, *Touching Our Strength: The Erotic as Power and Love of God* (San Francisco: Harper and Row, 1989), 42.

39. Ibid., 5-7.

40. Pope Leo XIII, Arcanum Divinae Sapientiae, in Odile M. Liebard, ed., *Official Catholic Teachings: Love and Sexuality* (1880; reprinted, Wilmington, NC: McGrath Publishing Company, 1978), 9.

41. Pope Pius XI, Casti Canubii, in Odile M. Liebard, ed., *Official Catholic Teachings: Love and Sexuality* (1930; reprinted, Wilmington, NC: McGrath Publishing Company, 1978), 35.

42. Ibid., 48.

43. The Reverend George A. Kelly, *The Catholic Marriage Manual* (New York: Random House, 1958), 6.

44. Pope John Paul II, On the Family: Familiaris Consortio (Rome: Vatican Council, 1981), 28.

CHAPTER 3

1. Rix Rogers, *Report of the Special Advisor to the Minister of National Health and Welfare on Child Sexual Abuse in Canada: Reaching For Solutions* (Ottawa: Ministry of Health and Welfare Canada, 1990), Cat. No. H74-28/1990E.

2. Canada, *Sexual Offenses Against Children: Report of the Committee on Sexual Offences Against Children and Youths,* Vol. 1, The Badgley Report (Ottawa: Ministry of Justice and Attorney General of Canada, Ministry of Health and Welfare, 1984) Cat. No. J 2-50/1984E.

3. Marilyn Callahan, "Feminist Approaches: Women Recreate Child Welfare," in Brian Wharf, ed., *Rethinking Child Welfare in Canada* (Toronto: McClelland and Stewart, 1993), 172-209; David Finkelhor, Gerald Hotaling, I. A. Lewis, and Christine Smith, "Sexual Abuse in a National Survey of Adult Men and Women: Prevalence, Characteristics, and Risk Factors," *Child Abuse and Neglect* 14, no. 1 (1990), 19-28; Marjorie Homer, Anne Leonard, and Pat Taylor, "The Burden of Dependency," in Norman Johnson, ed., *Marital Violence* (London: Routledge and Kegan Paul, 1985), 77-92; Rogers, *Reaching for Solutions;* and Florence Rush, *The Best Kept Secret: Sexual Abuse of Children* (Englewood Cliffs, NJ: Prentice-Hall, 1980).

4. Rogers, *Reaching for Solutions,* 17.

5. Ibid., 19.

6. Chris Bagley, "Mental Health and the In-Family Sexual Abuse of Children and Adolescents," in Benjamin Schlesinger, ed., *Sexual Abuse of Children in the 1980s* (Toronto: University of Toronto Press, 1986), 31.

7. See especially Chapter 2, "The Bible and the Talmud," and Chapter 3, "The Christians," in Florence Rush, *The Best Kept Secret.*

8. Annie Imbens and Ineke Jonker, *Christianity and Incest* (Minneapolis: Fortress Press, 1992), 3-4.

9. Mary DeYoung, "Women as Mothers and Wives in Paternally Incestuous Families: Coping with Role Conflict," *Child Abuse and Neglect* 18, no. 7 (1994), 73-83.

10. Ellen Bass and Laura Davis, *The Courage to Heal* (New York: Harper and Row, 1988).

11. Clare Davenport, Kevin Browne, and Robert Palmer, "Opinions on the Traumatizing Effects of Child Sexual Abuse: Evidence for Consensus," *Child Abuse and Neglect* 19, no. 18 (1994), 725-738; and Bass and Davis, *The Courage to Heal.*

12. Leslie Young, "Sexual Abuse and the Problem of Embodiment," *Child Abuse and Neglect* 16, no. 1 (1992), 88-100; Joseph H. Beitchman, Kenneth J. Zucker, Jane E. Hood, Granville A. DaCosta, Donna Akman and Erika Cassavia, "A Review of the Long-Term Effects of Child Sexual Abuse," *Child Abuse and Neglect* 16, no. 1 (1992), 101-118; Tamerra P. Moeller and Gloria A. Bachman, "The Combined Effects of Physical, Sexual and Emotional Abuse During Childhood: Long-Term Health Consequences for Women," *Child Abuse and Neglect* 17, no. 5 (1993), 623-640; and Jean Pierre Hotte and Sandra Rafman, "The Specific Effects of Incest on Prepubertal Girls from Dysfunctional Incest Families," *Child Abuse and Neglect* 16, no. 2 (1992), 273-283.

13. See, for example, Christopher Bagley, Michael Wood, and Loretta Young, "Victim to Abuser: Mental Health and Behavioral Sequels of Child Sexual Abuse in a Community Survey of Young Adult Males," *Child Abuse and Neglect* 18 no. 8 (1994), 683-697; and Myra Leifer, Jeremy P. Shapiro, and Layla Kassem, "The Impact of Maternal History and Behavior Upon Foster Placement and Adjustment in Sexually Abused Girls," *Child Abuse and Neglect* 17 no. 6 (1993), 755-766.

14. Young, "Sexual Abuse and the Problem of Embodiment."

15. See especially part one of Bass and Davis, *The Courage to Heal* which includes "Effects: Recognizing the Damage," 33-49, and "Coping: Honoring What You Did to Survive," 40-54.

16. Dorothy Smith, *The Conceptual Practices of Power* (Toronto: University of Toronto Press, 1990).

17. Herbert Maisch, *Incest* (New York: Stein and Day Publishers, 1972), 170, 176.

18. Robert F. Peterson, Samuel M. Basta, and Thane A. Dykstra, "Mothers of Molested Children: Some Comparisons of Personality Characteristics," *Child Abuse and Neglect* 17, no. 3 (1993), 409.

19. Liz Kelly, Linda Regan, and Sheila Burton, "Foreword," *No Right Way: The Voices of Mothers of Incest Survivors* (London: Scarlet Press, 1995), xiii.

20. Janis Tyler Johnson, *Mothers of Incest Survivors: Another Side of the Story* (Bloomington: Indiana University Press, 1992); see also Janet Liebman Jacobs, "Reassessing Mother Blame in Incest," *Signs* 15, no. 3 (1990), 500-514.

21. Tyler Johnson, *Mothers of Incest Survivors*, 15.

22. Ibid., 113.

23. Callahan, "Feminist Approaches."

24. For a typical example of pathology theory at work see an article by Dr. Judith V. Becker who, at the time of publication, was the director of the Sexual Abuse Behaviour Clinic, New York Psychiatric Institute. "Working with Perpetrators," in Kathleen Murray and David Gough, eds., *Intervening in Child Sexual Abuse* (Edinburgh: Scottish Academic Press, 1991), 157-165.

25. On the eroticization of female powerlessness and male aggression, see especially Mariana Valverde, *Sex, Power and Pleasure* (Toronto: Women's Press, 1985); and Sandra Lee Bartky, *Femininity and Domination: Studies in the Phenomenology of Oppression* (New York: Routledge, 1990).

26. Margrit Eichler, *Families in Canada Today: Recent Changes and Their Policy Consequences* (Toronto: Gage Educational Publishing Company, 1988), 39.

27. Carolyn Holderread Heggen, *Sexual Abuse in Christian Homes and Churches* (Scottdale, PA: Herald Press, 1993), 73.

28. Sandra Butler, *Conspiracy of Silence: The Trauma of Incest* (Volcano, CA: Volcano Press, 1985), 11. See also Carole R. Bohn, "Dominion to Rule: The Roots and Consequences of a Theology of Ownership," in Joanne Carlson Brown and Carole R. Bohn, eds., *Christianity, Patriarchy and Abuse* (New York: Pilgrim Press, 1989); Heggen, *Sexual Abuse in Christian Homes and Churches;* Imbens and Jonker, *Christianity and Incest.*

29. Morley Gunderson, Leon Muszynski, and Jennifer Keck, *Women and Labour Market Poverty* (Ottawa: Canadian Advisory Council on the Status of Women, 1990), Cat. No. LW31-32/1990E, 13.

30. Canada, "Violence Against Women Survey," *The Daily* (Ottawa: Statistics Canada, 1993), Cat. No. 11-001E.

31. Marjorie Homer, Anne Leonard, and Pat Taylor, "The Burden of Dependency," in Norman Johnson, ed., *Marital Violence* (London: Routledge and Kegan Paul, 1985), 72; see also Lee H. Bowker, Michelle Arbitell, J. Richard McFerron, "On the Relationship Between Wife Beating and Child Abuse," in Kersli Yllo and Michelle Bognad, eds., *Feminist Perspectives on Wife Abuse* (Newbury Park, CA: Sage Publications, 1988).

32. Eichler, *Families in Canada Today.*

33. Gunderson et al., *Women and Labour Market Poverty*, 82.

34. Callahan, "Feminist Approaches"; Gunderson et al., *Women and Labour Market Poverty.*

35. Michèle Barrett and Mary McIntosh, *The Anti-Social Family* (London: Verso, 1991).

36. Meg Luxton, "Two Hands for the Clock: Changing Patterns in the Gendered Division of Labour in the Home," in Meg Luxton, Harriet Rosenberg and Sedef Arat Koc, eds., *Through the Kitchen Window: The Politics of Home and Family* (Toronto: Garamond Press, 1990), 46.

CHAPTER 4

1. Mary Daly, "After the Death of God the Father," in Carol P. Christ and Judith Plaskow, eds., *Womanspirit Rising: A Feminist Reader in Religion* (San Francisco: HarperCollins, 1979), 54.

2. See, for example, Karen Anderson, *Chain Her by One Foot: The Subjugation of Women in Seventeenth-Century New France* (New York: Routledge, 1991); Joanne Carlson Brown and Carole R. Bohn, eds., *Christianity, Patriarchy and Abuse* (New York: Pilgrim Press, 1989); Mary Daly, *Beyond God the Father* (Boston: Beacon Press, 1973); Carolyn Holderread Heggen, *Sexual Abuse in Christian Homes and Churches* (Scottdale, PA: Herald Press, 1993); Uta Ranke-Heinemann, *Eunuchs for Heaven: The Catholic Church and Sexuality* (London: André Deutsch, 1990); and Eileen Zieget Silberman, *The Savage Sacrament: A Theology of Marriage After American Feminism* (Mystic, CT: Twenty-Third Publications, 1983).

3. Pope Pius XI, Casti Connubii, in Odile M. Liebard, ed., *Official Catholic Teachings: Love and Sexuality* (1930; reprint, Wilmington, NC: McGrath Publishing Company, 1978).

4. John Paul II, On the Family: Familiaris Consortio (Rome: Vatican Council, 1981), 28.

5. After the separation of the Christian church in the sixth century into East and West, "Catholic" was assumed as the descriptive epithet of the Western (or Roman) church, as "Orthodox" was of the Eastern (or Greek) church. During the Reformation in the late medieval period, the term "Catholic" was claimed as the exclusive right of the body remaining under the Roman obedience. *Oxford English Dictionary Compact Edition* (Oxford: Oxford University Press, 1977), 357.

6. Daly, *Beyond God the Father;* Daly, "After the Death of God the Father," 53-62; Ranke-Heinemann, *Eunuchs for Heaven.*

7. In medieval Europe, Christian philosophy dominated and the boundary between theology and philosophy was nearly non-existent. See, for example, Armand A. Maurer, *Medieval Philosophy* (Toronto: Pontifical Institute of Medieval Studies, 1962 [1982]).

8. Ibid.; Ranke-Heinemann, *Eunuchs for Heaven.*

9. Augustine, as cited in Ranke-Heinemann, *Eunuchs for Heaven,* 77.

10. Ranke-Heinemann, *Eunuchs for Heaven,* 62.

11. Ibid., 163.

12. Thomas Aquinas, cited in Ranke-Heinemann, *Eunuchs for Heaven,* 73.

13. Albertus Magnus, cited in Ranke-Heinemann, *Eunuchs for Heaven,* 157.

14. Daly, *Beyond God the Father,* 81.

15. Ranke-Heinemann, *Eunuchs for Heaven,* 311.

16. Pope John Paul II, Familiaris Consortio: On the Family, 28.

17. Daly, *Beyond God the Father,* 49.

18. Rosemary Radford Ruether, "The Western Religious Tradition and Violence Against Women in the Home," in Brown and Bohn, eds., *Christianity, Patriarchy and Abuse,* 36.

19. Eleanor Leacock, "Montagnais Women and the Jesuit Program for Colonization," in Veronica Strong-Boag and Anita Clair Fellman, eds., *Rethinking Canada: The Promise of Women's History* (Toronto: Copp Clark-Pitman, 1991), 7-22.

20. Anderson, *Chain Her by One Foot,* 97-98.

21. Sylvia Hale, "Social Cohesion and Order," in Hale, ed., *Controversies in Canadian Sociology* (Toronto: Copp Clark-Pitman, 1990), 175.

22. News release, *Evening Telegram* (St. John's, NF), 21 March 1995.

23. Margrit Eichler, *The Pro-Family Movement: Are They For or Against Families?* (Ottawa: Canadian Research Institute for the Advancement of Women, 1985).

24. "Christian Men's Movement Attracts Interest in St. John's," *Evening Telegram* (St. John's, NF), 23 April 1997.

25. Radford Ruether, "The Western Religious Tradition and Violence Against Women in the Home," 38, 39.

CHAPTER 5

1. Dorothy Smith, *The Conceptual Practices of Power* (Toronto: Toronto University Press, 1990), 11 [emphasis added].

2. See, for example, Mary Jo Leddy, Douglas Roche, and Bishop Remi De Roo, *In the Eye of the Catholic Storm: The Church Since Vatican II* (Toronto: HarperCollins, 1992); and the epilogue in Terrence Murphy, ed., *A Concise History of Christianity in Canada* (Toronto: Oxford University Press, 1996).

3. Gillian Walker, *Family Violence and the Women's Movement: The Conceptual Politics of Struggle* (Toronto: University of Toronto Press, 1990), 9.

4. Louise Dulude, "Outline of Matrimonial Property Laws in Canada" (Ottawa: Canadian Advisory Council on the Status of Women, 1982), i.

5. Charles Panati, *Panati's Parade of Fads, Follies and Manias* (New York: HarperCollins, 1991), 307.

6. Adrienne Rich, "Compulsory Heterosexuality and Lesbian Existence," *Signs* 5 (1980), 631-660.

7. Mary Daly expresses a similar view in *Beyond God the Father* (Boston: Beacon Press, 1973).

8. Karl Rahner and Herbert Vorgrimler, *Theological Dictionary* (New York: Herder and Herder, 1965); Leddy et al., *In the Eye of the Catholic Storm*.

9. Two examples of this shift in the post–Vatican II language are relevant. First, Pope John Paul II uses inclusive language although such inclusive language is limited to discussion of female and male human beings — God imagery remains masculine. Second, his 1981 exhortation on marriage and the family, in the spirit of openness that characterized the implementation of Vatican II, invites the contributions of social scientific research. However, a qualifying clause renders questionable the value the Pope would give, for example, to this book. He writes: "The church values sociological and statistical research ... when it leads to a better understanding of the truth" (24). Since I identify the church's teachings as ideology this book would probably not be considered an enhancement of "the truth." Ideology implies relativism — the notion that what is "true" shifts over time — which the church "deplores." The church's position, however, ignores the ways in which Catholicism's "truths" have been enforced and shaped over time by an unquestionably patriarchal ruling apparatus.

10. Alison M. Jaggar, "Political Philosophies of Women's Liberation," in Laurel Richardson and Verta Taylor, eds., *Feminist Frontiers: Rethinking Sex, Gender and Society* (Reading, MA: Addison-Wesley, 1983), 322.

11. Pope John Paul II, Familiaris Consortio: On the Family (Rome: Vatican Council, 1981), 28.

12. Leddy et al., *In the Eye of the Catholic Storm*, 62-63.

13. See, for example, Sally Cole, *Women of the Praia: Work and Lives in a Portuguese Coastal Community* (Princeton, NJ: Princeton University Press, 1991), 82.

14. Dorothy E. Smith, *The Everyday World as Problematic* (Boston: Northeastern University Press, 1987), 55, 57.

15. Smith, *The Conceptual Practices of Power*, 13.

16. Ellen Bass and Laura Davis, *The Courage to Heal* (New York: Harper and Row, 1988); Joseph H. Beitchman, Kenneth J. Zucker, Jane E. Hood, Granville A. DaCosta, Donna Akman, and Erika Cassavia, "A Review of the Long-Term Effects of Child Sexual Abuse," *Child Abuse and Neglect* 16, no. 1 (1992), 101-118; Leslie Young, "Sexual Abuse and the Problem of Embodiment," *Child Abuse and Neglect* 16, no. 1 (1992), 88-100.

17. Smith, *The Conceptual Practices of Power*, 12.

18. Ibid., 11.

CHAPTER 6

1. The Reverend George A. Kelly, *The Catholic Marriage Manual* (New York: Random House, 1958), 6.

2. Pope Leo XIII, Arcanum Divinae Sapientae, in Odile M. Liebard, ed., *Official Catholic Teachings: Love and Sexuality* (1880; reprinted, Wilmington, NC: McGrath Publishing Company, 1978), 6.

3. Kelly, *The Catholic Marriage Manual,* 25.

4. Personal communication with Jordan Bishop, retired former professor of the humanities, University College of Cape Breton (Sydney, NS), June 3, 1997.

5. Kelly, *The Catholic Marriage Manual,* 6.

6. Ibid., 25, 26.

7. Pope Leo XIII, Arcanum Divinae Sapientae, 6.

8. Pope John Paul II, On the Family: Familiaris Consortio (Rome: Vatican Council, 1981), 28.

9. Ibid., 29.

10. Ibid., 24, 25.

11. Ibid., 28.

12. Mary Daly, "After the Death of God the Father," in Carol P. Christ and Judith Plaskow, eds., *Womanspirit Rising: A Feminist Reader in Religion* (San Francisco: HarperCollins, 1979), 54.

13. Pope John Paul II, On the Family, 29.

CHAPTER 7

1. Pope John Paul II, On the Family: Familiaris Consortio (Rome: Vatican Council, 1981), 28.

2. Pope Pius XI, Casti Connubii, in Odile M. Liebard, ed., *Official Catholic Teachings: Love and Sexuality* (1930), 47, 48.

3. The Reverend George A. Kelly, *The Catholic Marriage Manual* (New York: Random House, 1958), 25.

4. Ibid., 16.

5. Pope John Paul II, On the Family, 28-29.

6. See, for example, Marilyn Callahan, "Feminist Approaches: Women Recreate Child Welfare," in Brian Wharf, ed., *Rethinking Child Welfare in Canada* (Toronto: McClelland and Stewart, 1993), 172-209; Meg Luxton, Harriet Rosenberg, and Sedef Arat Koc, eds., *Through the Kitchen Window: The Politics of Home and Family* (Toronto: Garamond Press, 1990).

7. Such social supports remain largely unavailable to mothers in Canadian society.

8. Kelly, *The Catholic Marriage Manual*, 25.

CHAPTER 8

1. John Paul II, Familiaris Consortio: On the Family (Rome: Vatican Council, 1981), 25.

2. Ibid.

3. Sally Cole, *Women of the Praia: Work and Lives in a Portuguese Coastal Community* (Princeton, NJ: Princeton University Press, 1991).

4. This claim is well supported by other feminist scholars. See, for example, Carol J. Adams and Marie M. Fortune, *Violence Against Women and Children: A Christian Theological Sourcebook* (New York: Continuum Publishing Company, 1995); Karen Anderson, *Chain Her by One Foot: The Subjugation of Women in Seventeenth-Century New France* (New York: Routledge, 1991); Joanne Carlson Brown and Carole R. Bohn, eds., *Christianity, Patriarchy and Abuse* (New York: Pilgrim Press, 1989); Mary Daly, *Beyond God the Father* (Boston: Beacon Press, 1973); Carolyn Holderread Heggen, *Sexual Abuse in Christian Homes and Churches* (Scottdale, PA: Herald Press, 1993); Uta Ranke-Heinemann, *Eunuchs for Heaven: The Catholic Church and Sexuality* (London: André Deutsch, 1990); and Eileen Zieget Silberman, *The Savage Sacrament: A Theology of Marriage After American Feminism* (Mystic, CT: Twenty-Third Publications, 1983).

5. Carter Heyward, *Touching Our Strength: The Erotic as Power and the Love of God* (San Francisco: Harper and Row, 1989).

6. For more on the distinction between mortal and venial sins, see, for example, Karl Rahner and Herbert Vorgrimler's *Theological Dictionary* (New York: Herder and Herder, 1965), 436.

7. Dorothy Smith, *The Everyday World as Problematic* (Boston: Northeastern University Press, 1987).

8. Sheila A. Redmond, "Christian 'Virtues' and Recovery from Child Sexual Abuse," in Joanne Carlson Brown and Carole R. Bohn, eds., *Christianity, Patriarchy and Abuse* (New York: Pilgrim Press, 1989), 74.

CHAPTER 9

1. John Paul II, Familiaris Consortio: On the Family (Rome: Vatican Council, 1981), 23.

2. Recall a guiding principle of feminist standpoint theory, that women's struggles against oppression provide women with an epistemically privileged perspective on the social world. See especially Sandra Harding, "Rethinking Standpoint Epistemology: What Is 'Strong Objectivity'?," in Elizabeth Potter and Linda Alcoff, eds., *Feminist Epistemologies* (New York: Routledge, Chapman and Hall, 1993), 49–82; and Sandra Harding, "Starting Thought from Women's Lives: Eight Points for Maximizing Objectivity," *Journal of Social Philosophy* 21, nos. 2/3 (1991).

3. Dorothy Smith, *The Conceptual Practices of Power* (Toronto: University of Toronto Press, 1990), 11.

4. See, for example, Marilyn Callahan, "Feminist Approaches: Women Recreate Child Welfare," in Brian Wharf, ed., *Rethinking Child Welfare in Canada* (Toronto: McClelland and Stewart, 1993); Mary Daly, "After the Death of God the Father," in Carol P. Christ and Judith Plaskow, eds., *Womanspirit Rising: A Feminist Reader in Religion* (San Francisco: Harper-Collins, 1979), 53–62; Mary Daly, *Beyond God the Father* (Boston: Beacon Press, 1973); Carter Heyward, *Touching Our Strength: The Erotic as Power and the Love of God* (San Francisco: Harper and Row, 1989); and Florence Rush, *The Best Kept Secret: Sexual Abuse of Children* (New Jersey: Prentice-Hall, 1982).

5. Michèle Barrett and Mary McIntosh, *The Anti-Social Family* (London: Verso, 1991).

6. Ibid.

7. Heyward, *Touching Our Strength.*

8. Michael T. Ryan, *Solidarity: Christian Social Teaching and Canadian Society* (London, ON: Guided Study Programs in the Catholic Faith, 1990).

9. Heyward, *Touching Our Strength*, 4.

GLOSSARY

NOTE TO READERS: The glossary defines terms as they are used in this book. "Ideology," for example, means other things in other contexts.

Alienation: A psychological state, resulting from the relation between women's activities and an external order that oppresses them, in which women's activities strengthen that order; also, a psychological state in which a woman/girl is cut off from her actual everyday/everynight experiences.

Capitalism: The dominant economic system in the western world, based on competition in the marketplace, ownership of capital and exploitation of labour.

Catholic Family Ideology: Ideas and practices based on Catholic teachings that assign to men in families a position of social privilege and to women responsibility for childcare and domestic labour.

Catholic Sexual Ideology: Ideas and practices based on the Catholic teaching that sexuality belongs only in marriage between heterosexual, monogamous spouses for procreative purposes; it defines the parameters for "morally appropriate" sexual relations.

Dissociation: An involuntary "split" between actual events and one's conscious awareness of a traumatic episode; also, the involuntary act of repressing memories after a traumatic episode. (See also Repressed Memories.)

Epistemology: Derived from the Greek *episteme,* meaning knowledge; a study of the origins and limits of human knowledge; in this book, a feminist epistemology is used to study the social construction of knowledge about Catholic family culture from the standpoint of women.

Feminist Participatory Action Research: A research methodology that makes research participants central rather than peripheral actors in the discovery/production of knowledge; assumes that social change is an important goal of research.

Feminist Praxis: The joining of theory and action in order to challenge gender and sexual oppression; the dynamic interplay between feminist theory and practice.

Feminist Standpoint Theory: An epistemology grounded in the Hegelian and Marxist traditions that assumes that women who both experience and struggle against oppression can "know" the world in less distorted ways than those who have interests in maintaining the status quo. (See also Standpoint Of Women.)

Gender and Sexual Relations: Relations between women/girls and men/boys that are shaped by societal institutions (e.g. the media, the legal/justice system, patriarchal religions, etc.).

Honour and Shame Code: A system of social control in which a community rewards and punishes its members according to set of unambiguous standards.

Ideology: Patriarchal ideas and their concomitant practices that underpin and sanction our societal institutions, including religious institutions.

Incest: Includes a continuum of sexual acts and contacts initiated by (usually adult, usually male) family members (e.g. father, stepfather, uncle, grandfather, mother, etc.) in which the wishes of the child are not taken into account.

Institution of Compulsory Heterosexuality: The enforcement of heterosexuality through a variety of social practices; exemplified by an indissoluble, monogamous bond between spouses in which a woman is economically dependent on her husband.

Lines of Fault/Fault Lines: Ruptures/disjunctures in women's everyday/everynight experiences within a world ordered and constructed by men; in this book, ruptures/disjunctures between *idealized* Catholic family life and Catholic families as they were *actually* experienced by women.

Material Conditions: Economic and structural conditions that change over time and shape people's choices in their everyday/everynight lives.

Mother-Blaming: Also called "maternal collusion," a theory explaining incest that assumes a mother either colludes in the incest to avoid sex with her husband/male partner or fails to assume a "proper" sexual role thereby forcing the role onto her daughter.

Pathology Theory: A theory explaining sexual abuse that assumes perpetrators are committing deviant, antisocial acts that most "normal" and "strong-willed" people will not commit; looks to the individual perpetrator or family for the source of "sickness" or "dysfunction."

Patriarchy: A system of ideas and practices that privilege men over women and children.

Positivism: An epistemology that acknowledges empirical observation and logic as the only valid sources of knowledge; strives to produce "objective" and politically neutral results.

Repressed Memories: A primary coping mechanism after a traumatic episode in which knowledge of the trauma is blocked from consciousness. (See also Dissociation.)

Second-Wave Feminism: The women's liberation movement beginning in the 1960s whose advocates adopted the dictum "the personal is political" and politicized (among other things) gender and sexual relations within the private sphere; first-wave feminism emerged in the 1880s.

Sexual Justice: A dimension of social justice that links patterns of gender and sexual injustice to those of economic, political and racial injustice.

Social Justice: A guiding principle of social movements that seek to alleviate injustice in its many forms (economic, political, racial, etc.).

Socialist Feminism: A theory of women's liberation that combines Marxist/materialist feminism and radical feminism; emphasizes women's economic powerlessness in society and criticizes practices that enforce the institution of compulsory heterosexuality.

Standpoint of Women: A critical perspective on the world emerging from women's awareness of ruptures/disjunctures in their everyday/everynight lives. (See also Feminist Standpoint Theory.)

Theoretical Framework: In social research, a body of theory that provides a way of understanding everyday/everynight events.

Vatican II/Second Vatican Council: A council of the official Catholic church that met between 1959 and 1965 and endeavoured to bring Catholicism up to date with contemporary culture.

SELECTED BIBLIOGRAPHY

Adams, Carol J., and Marie M. Fortune. *Violence Against Women and Children: A Christian Theological Sourcebook.* New York: Continuum Publishing Company, 1995.

Anderson, Karen. *Chain Her by One Foot: The Subjugation of Women in Seventeenth-Century New France.* New York: Routledge, 1991.

Atlantis: A Women's Studies Journal/Revue d'Etudes Sur les Femmes. 21, no.1.(Fall/Automne 1996) Special Issue: "Connecting Practices, Doing Theory."

Bagley, Chris. "Mental Health and the In-Family Sexual Abuse of Children and Adolescents." In *Sexual Abuse of Children in the 1980s,* edited by Benjamin Schlesinger, 30-50. Toronto: University of Toronto Press, 1986.

Bagley, Christopher, Michael Wood, and Loretta Young. "Victim to Abuser: Mental Health and Behavioral Sequels of Child Sexual Abuse in a Community Survey of Young Adult Males." *Child Abuse and Neglect* 18, no. 8 (1994): 683-697.

Barrett, Michèle, and Mary McIntosh. *The Anti-Social Family.* London: Verso, 1991.

Bartky, Sandra Lee. *Femininity and Domination: Studies in the Phenomenology of Oppression.* New York: Routledge, Chapman and Hall, 1990.

Bass, Ellen, and Laura Davis. *The Courage to Heal.* New York: Fitzhenry and Whiteside, 1988.

Beitchman, Joseph H., Kenneth J. Zucker, Jane E. Hood, Granville A. DaCosta, Donna Akman, and Erika Cassavia. "A Review of the Long-Term Effects of Child Sexual Abuse." *Child Abuse and Neglect* 16, no. 1 (1992): 101-118.

Brookes, Ann Louise. *Feminist Pedagogy: An Autobiographical Approach.* Halifax: Fernwood, 1992.

Butler, Sandra. *Conspiracy of Silence: The Trauma of Incest.* Volcano, CA: Volcano Press, 1978.

Callahan, Marilyn. "Feminist Approaches: Women Recreate Child Welfare in Canada." In *Rethinking Child Welfare in Canada,* edited by Brian Wharf, 172-209. Toronto: McClelland and Stewart, 1993.

Campbell, Marie, and Ann Manicom, eds. *Knowledge, Experience, and Ruling Relations: Studies in the Social Organization of Knowledge.* Toronto: University of Toronto Press, 1995.

Canada. *The Badgley Report: Sexual Offences Against Children: Report of the Committee on Sexual Offences Against Children and Youths,* Vol. 1. Ottawa: Ministry of Justice and Attorney General of Canada, Ministry of Health and Welfare, 1984. Cat. No. J 2-50/1984E.

Canadian Conference of Catholic Bishops. *From Pain to Hope: Report from the CCCB Ad Hoc Committee on Child Sexual Abuse.* Ottawa: CCCB, 1992.

Carlson Brown, Joanne, and Carole R. Bohn, eds. *Christianity, Patriarchy and Abuse.* New York: Pilgrim Press, 1989.

Cole, Sally. *Women of the Praia: Work and Lives in a Portuguese Coastal Community.* Princeton, NJ: Princeton University Press, 1991.

Daly, Mary. "After the Death of God the Father." In *Womanspirit Rising: A Feminist Reader in Religion,* edited by Carol P. Christ and Judith Plaskow, 53-62. San Francisco: HarperCollins, 1979.

―――. *Beyond God the Father.* Boston: Beacon Press, 1973.

Desroches, Leonard. *Allow the Water: Anger, Fear, Power, Work, Sexuality, Community — and the Spirituality and Practice of Non-Violence.* Toronto: Dunamis Publishers, 1996.

Dulude, Louise. "Outline of Matrimonial Property Laws in Canada." Ottawa: Canadian Advisory Council on the Status of Women, 1982.

Eichler, Margrit. *Families in Canada Today: Recent Changes and Their Policy Implications.* Toronto: Gage Educational Publishing Company, 1988.

―――. "The Pro-Family Movement: Are They For or Against Families?" Ottawa: Canadian Research Institute for the Advancement of Women (CRIAW), 1985.

Finkelhor, David, R. J. Gelles, Gerald T. Hotaling, and Murray A. Straus, eds. *The Dark Side of Families: Current Family Violence Research.* London: Sage Publications, 1983.

Finkelhor, David, Gerald Hotaling, I. A. Lewis, and Christine Smith. "Sexual Abuse in a National Survey of Adult Men and Women: Prevalence, Characteristics and Risk Factors." *Child Abuse and Neglect* 14, no. 1 (1990): 19-28.

Foote Whyte, William, ed. *Participatory Action Research.* Newbury Park, CA: Sage Publications, 1991.

Freire, Paulo. *Pedagogy of the Oppressed.* New York: Herder and Herder, 1971.

Gilson, Anne Bathurst. *Eros Breaking Free: Interpreting Sexual Theo-Ethics.* Cleveland: The Pilgrim Press, 1995.

Gunderson, Morley, and Leon Muszynski, with Jennifer Keck. *Women and Labour Market Poverty.* Ottawa: Canadian Advisory Council on the Status of Women, 1990.

Hale, Sylvia. "Social Cohesion and Order." *In Controversies in Canadian Sociology: A Canadian Introduction,* edited by Sylvia Hale, 172-178. Toronto: Copp Clark-Pitman, 1990.

Harding, Sandra. "Rethinking Standpoint Epistemology: What Is 'Strong Objectivity'?" In *Feminist Epistemologies,* edited by Elizabeth Potter and Linda Alcoff, 49-82. New York: Routledge, Chapman and Hall, 1993.

———. *The Science Question in Feminism.* Ithaca: Cornell University Press, 1986.

———. "Starting Thought From Women's Lives: Eight Points for Maximizing Objectivity." *Journal of Social Philosophy* 21, no. 2/3 (1991): 141-149.

———. *Whose Science? Whose Knowledge? Thinking from Women's Lives.* Ithaca: Cornell University Press, 1991.

Hartsock, Nancy. "The Feminist Standpoint: Developing the Ground for a Specifically Feminist Historical Materialism." In *Discovering Reality,* edited by Sandra Harding and Merrill B. Hintikka, 283-310. London: D. Reidel Publishing Company, 1983.

Heyward, Carter. *Touching Our Strength: The Erotic as Power and the Love of God.* San Francisco: Harper and Row, 1989.

Holderread Heggan, Carolyn. *Sexual Abuse in Christian Homes and Churches.* Scottdale, PA: Herald Press, 1993.

Homer, Marjorie, Anne Leonard, and Pat Taylor. "The Burden of Dependency." In *Marital Violence,* edited by Norman Johnson, 77-92. London: Routledge and Kegan Paul, 1985.

Hotte, Jean Pierre, and Sandra Rafman. "The Specific Effects of Incest on Prepubertal Girls from Dysfunctional Incest Families." *Child Abuse and Neglect* 16, no. 2 (1992): 273-283.

Imbens, Annie, and Ineke Jonker. *Christianity and Incest.* Minneapolis: Fortress Press, 1992.

Jaggar, Alison M. *Feminist Politics and Human Nature.* Totowa, NJ: Rowman and Littlefield Publishers, 1988.

John Paul II (Pope). On the Family: Familiaris Consortio. Rome: Vatican Council, 1981.

Kessler, Susan J., and Wendy McKenna. *Gender: An Ethnomethodological Approach.* Chicago: University of Chicago Press, 1978.

Kirby, Sandra, and Kate McKenna. *Experience, Research, Social Change: Methods From the Margins.* Toronto: Garamond Press, 1989.

Leddy, Mary Jo, Douglas Roche, and Bishop Remi De Roo. *In the Eye of the Storm: The Church Since Vatican II.* Toronto: HarperCollins, 1992.

Leifer, Myra, Jeremy P. Shapiro, and Layla Kassem. "The Impact of Maternal History and Behavior upon Foster Placement and Adjustment in Sexually Abused Girls." *Child Abuse and Neglect* 17, no. 6 (1993): 755-766.

Liebard, Odile M. *Official Catholic Teachings: Love and Sexuality.* Wilmington, NC: McGrath Publishing Company, 1978.

Luxton, Meg, Harriet Rosenberg, and Sedef Arat Koc, eds. *Through the Kitchen Window: The Politics of Home and Family.* Toronto: Garamond Press, 1990.

Maguire, Patricia. *Doing Participatory Research: A Feminist Approach.* Amherst, MA: Centre for International Education, 1987.

Marshall, Catherine, and Gretchen B. Rossman. *Designing Qualitative Research.* Newbury Park, CA: Sage Publications, 1989.

Millett, Kate. "Sexual Politics: A Manifesto for Revolution." In *Radical Feminism,* edited by Anne Koedt, Ellen Levine and Anita Rapone, 365-367. New York: Quadrangle Books, 1973.

Moeller, Tamerra P., and Gloria A. Bachman. "The Combined Effects of Physical, Sexual and Emotional Abuse during Childhood: Long-Term Health Consequences for Women." *Child Abuse and Neglect* 17, no. 5 (1993): 623-640.

Morgan, David L. *Focus Groups as Qualitative Research.* Newbury Park, CA: Sage Publications, 1988.

Orr, Tracy. *No Right Way: The Voices of Mothers of Incest Survivors.* London: Scarlet Press, 1995.

Peterson, Robert F., Samuel M. Basta, and Thane A. Dykstra. "Mothers of Molested Children: Some Comparisons of Personality Characteristics." *Child Abuse and Neglect* 17, no. 4 (1993): 409-418.

Radicalesbians. "The Woman Identified Woman." In *Radical Feminism,* edited by Anne Koedt, Ellen Levine and Anita Rapone, 240-245. New York: Quadrangle Books, 1973.

Ranke-Heinemann, Uta. *Eunuchs for Heaven: The Catholic Church and Sexuality.* London: André Deutsch, 1990.

Reinharz, Shulamit. *Feminist Methods in Social Research.* New York: Oxford University Press, 1992.

Rich, Adrienne. "Compulsory Heterosexuality and Lesbian Existence." *Signs* 5 (1980): 631-660.

Ristock, Janice L. and Joan Pennell. *Community Research as Empowerment: Feminist Links, Postmodern Interruptions.* Toronto: Oxford University Press, 1996.

Rogers, Rix. *Report of the Special Advisor to the Minister of National Health and Welfare on Child Sexual Abuse in Canada: Reaching for Solutions.* Ottawa: Ministry of Health and Welfare Canada, 1990.

Rush, Florence. *The Best Kept Secret: Sexual Abuse of Children.* Englewood Cliffs, NJ: Prentice-Hall, 1980.

Ryan, Michael T. *Solidarity: Christian Social Teaching and Canadian Society.* London, ON: Guided Study Programs in the Catholic Faith, 1990.

Smith, Dorothy E. *The Conceptual Practices of Power.* Toronto: University of Toronto Press, 1990.

―――. *The Everyday World as Problematic.* Boston: Northeastern University Press, 1987.

Tyler Johnson, Janis. *Mothers of Incest Survivors: Another Side of the Story.* Indianapolis: Indiana University press, 1992.

Walker, Gillian. *Family Violence and the Women's Movement: The Conceptual Politics of Struggle.* Toronto: University of Toronto Press, 1990.

The Winter Commission. *The Report of the Archdiocesan Commission of Enquiry in the Sexual Abuse of Children by Members of the Clergy.* St. John's, NF: Archdiocese of St. John's, 1990.

Young, Leslie. "Sexual Abuse and the Problem of Embodiment." *Child Abuse and Neglect* 16 no.1 (1992): 88-100.

Zieget Silberman, Eileen. *The Savage Sacrament: A Theology of Marriage after American Feminism.* Mystic, CT: Twenty-Third Publications, 1983.

Index

gendered division of labour 183
  in Catholic family culture 14, 42,
    97, 123-124, 141, 142-143, 184-
    185
  in Catholic theology 99, 139, 141-
    142
  and compulsory heterosexuality 59
  and family violence 80-81, 83-85
  see also socio-economic conditions
    for mothers
grandfathers 73
grandmothers 17, 165, 166

Harding, Sandra 22-23, 23
  feminist standpoint theory 56, 60,
    61-63
Harstock, Nancy 56, 60, 62
health
  lont-term effects of incest 40, 78
Hegel, Georg Wilhelm Friedrich 61
Heggen, Carolyn Holderread 82
Heyward, Carter 56, 160
  sexual justice theory 11, 19, 68
  theology of 13
historical materialism 59
  and emergence of fault lines 66-67,
    103-104, 109-115
  see also material conditions; socio-
    economic conditions for mothers
Holy Communion 159, 162-163, 163,
  180-181
honour and shame code 109-110, 159-
  160, 160-167, 219
  for Catholic wives 149-151
Huron 97
husbands 68, 120, 173-174
  fear of 132
  as head of family 69

ideology 12-13, 23, 61, 65, 219
see also Catholic ideology; Catholic family ideology; Catholic patriarchal
  ideology; Catholic sexual ideology;

patriarchal ideology; religious
  ideology
Imbens, Annie 73
incest 73, 219
  as betrayal of trust 74-75
  as breach of honour and shame code
    160-167, 170-172
  family environment and 73-74, 83-
    85
  feminist theory of 82
  historical roots of in Catholic fami-
    lies 15-16
  history of as fault line 102-115
  intergenerational patterns of 76-77,
    151-154
  long-term consequences of 75-76
  maternal collusion theory of 79-81,
    139
  mothers' denial of 74-75, 137, 138,
    147-148
  pathology theory of 81-82
  repressing memories of 77-79, 101
  secrecy of 167-170
  as sexual abuse of children 71-72
  as sexual oppression 13-14, 63
  social awareness of 101-102, 145-
    146
  see also sexual abuse of children
incest survivors
  emergence of critical standpoint
    102-115
  experience of body shame 164, 166,
    172-173
  feminist standpoint theory of 61,
    63, 69-70
  identification with Eve 93-94
  secrecy and silence 167-170
  self-esteem 96, 160-163
  shame 165-167
  see also Cherrie, Content, Courage,
    Elizabeth, Faye, Jackie, Mary,
    Maya

long-term consequences of 75-79
patriarchal roots of 71, 72-73
social awareness of 101-102, 145-146
see also incest
sexual division of labour 60
see also gendered division of labour
sexual justice 11, 19-20, 32, 68, 220
social justice and 20-22, 56, 188
sexuality
in Catholic ideology 89-91, 157
Catholic teachings on 18-19, 157-158
Virgin Mary as model of 92-94, 109, 150, 150-151
sexual purity and self-esteem 95-96
women's actual experiences of 70, 87, 159-174
women's reclaiming of 181, 185, 185-186
see also Catholic sexual ideology; shame; sins, sexual
shame 40
honour and shame codes 109-110, 149-151, 159
sexual shame 161-167
sins, sexual 161, 162-163, 163, 163-164, 165-166
redefining 185-186
Smith, Dorothy E. 22-23, 23, 78, 101, 103, 105, 111, 114, 148, 167
feminist standpoint theory 56, 57, 60, 61, 63-65, 66
social justice 220
feminist application of 32
teachings of Catholic church 17-18
sexual justice and 20-22, 56, 188
socialist-feminism 22, 55, 55-56, 56, 57-59, 220
socialist-feminist
analysis of gendered division of labour 84-85

analysis of socio-economic conditions of mothers 138-148
socio-economic conditions of mothers 83-85, 183
in Catholic families 115
during pre-Vatican II 104
during second-wave feminism 103, 112
for mothers of incest families 79-81, 138, 148, 154-155
standpoint of women 220
critique of Catholic culture 88-89
emergence of 102-115
for incest survivors 56, 69-70
in research methodology 32, 48-49
see also feminist standpoint theory; incest survivors
stepfathers 43, 73, 75, 125, 130, 146

theology
vs ideology 13, 187
women's moral inferiority 89-91
women's role in marriage and family 68-70
Touching Our Strength: The Erotic as Power and the Love of God (Heyward) 68
trust
betrayal of 74-75, 76

uncles 73, 77, 124-125, 125, 128, 168

Vatican II 220
post: 69, 99
awareness of family violence 102-103, 108, 112-113
influence of on family culture 102-103, 106-108
sexual ideology and women's experiences 157, 158, 160-161, 166-167, 167-168, 168-169, 173-174
women participants 29, 34